POWERFUL
FEMALE IMMIGRANTS
WHO INSPIRE GREATNESS

VOLUME 2

24 Women
Stories
Movement

Quantity sales and special discounts are available on quantity purchases by corporations, associations, and others. For details, contact the publisher at the address above.

Orders by U.S. trade bookstores and wholesalers. Email info@ BeyondPublishing.net

The Beyond Publishing Speakers Bureau can bring authors to your live event. For more information or to book an event contact the Beyond Publishing Speakers Bureau speak@BeyondPublishing.net

The Author can be reached directly at BeyondPublishing.net

Manufactured and printed in the United States of America distributed globally by BeyondPublishing.net

BEYOND
PUBLISHING

New York | Los Angeles | London | Sydney

ISBN Softcover: 978-1-63792-561-4
ISBN Hardcover: 978-1-63792-560-7

Hope you enjoy
reading this book!

5. 8. 23

TABLE OF CONTENTS

POWERFUL
FEMALE IMMIGRANTS
WHO INSPIRE GREATNESS

POWERFUL FEMALE IMMIGRANTS

Foreword- By Julie Schaecher

My father immigrated to this country from Mexico in the 1950's. He was one of the oldest of twelve children whose mother had been abandoned by their father leaving them without care. Upon arrival in the US, they slept in a chicken coup and ate meals cooked over an open fire.

Flash forward, I am sitting in the living room of a Nigerian governor's estate where I was invited to stay while I worked as a liaison for their tourism department and the thought running through my mind is, "What in the world happened in our family to take them from a chicken coup to a governor's estate in one generation?" I

It all begins with my grandmother, a powerful female immigrant who refused to believe that living in abject poverty, hoping that the people around her would care for and provide for her and her children was the best she could do. She courageously took her future into her own hands and executed a plan to get her family to America where she believed they had a chance to make a decent life for themselves. Everyone around her told her it was impossible but she believed she could, and so she did.

She would spend her life working in the janitorial department of our local hospital. Along with the help of her three oldest children, my dad being one of them, she was able to provide for her family, buy a home, and ensure that all her children were cared for and loved.

Many of my uncles and aunts grew up to enjoy both personal and professional success. We all marveled when my aunt, the youngest of the twelve, was honored at the White House for being one of Americas distinguished minority businesswomen. It was proof that one woman, making one courageous decision to follow her dreams, can drastically change the future of generations to come.

I remember weeping as I watched my dad cheer for my daughter, his youngest granddaughter, as she received her master's degree in Speech Pathology. He never had the opportunity to finish school and barely had an eighth-grade education but, he had been honored to watch every single one of his grandchildren graduate from college. The pride in his eyes and smile on his face tells the story of how quickly things can turn around. In our family it began with one powerful female immigrant embracing her seemingly impossible dream of a better life.

Michael Butler has assembled an inspiring collection of similar stories from powerful female immigrants who have embraced their God inspired destinies and stepped into their areas of influence with courage and fortitude. These women are making a difference for this generation and for generations to come.

I was recently in a country where women are highly oppressed and often persecuted for even having a desire to go to school. I was there to do a women's leadership conference. One of the young women that I brought with me had just finished speaking from the stage when she was approached by a young lady who had been sitting in the front row. With tears streaming from her eyes she says, "From the time that I was born, I knew that I was called as a leader to the nations. Everyone told me, that it was impossible, but now that I have seen you, I know that I can do it. "

It is important for the voices of the women in this book to be released and for their stories to be told. Their testimonies will ignite hope, light a fire in our hearts and dare us to dream of impossible things.

We now celebrate them and gladly learn from their powerful examples.

Pastor Julie Schaecher

Author, International Speaker, Life Strategies Consultant

Founder of The Now Conference-Global Women's Leadership Movement

Founding Board Member 1040Impact.org

INTRODUCTION

Michael D. Butler

For years I've been amazed at immigrants in general and female immigrants in particular. Having traveled to speak in 30 countries I see the passion and the fire in these Powerful Female Immigrants, not just to succeed but to thrive and bring a legacy to future generations.

They are like the women who settled America in the early days as they traveled west in their covered wagons, while the men built saloons and brothels the women started schools and churches. Women, the true nurturers, the women of wisdom like Proverbs 31 speaks of who build several businesses for their family to have multiple income streams as they work from home, guide the house and show their children and their entire neighborhood not just with words but by example, how life can be lived honorably and powerfully.

They go about their daily tasks, rising before sunrise, preparing their kids and their family and their businesses for success. Never seeking recognition or applause, their work is done behind the scenes and in the shadows, when no one is watching. But, yes someone is watching. Someone notices, and we want to honor all of the women in this book with their amazing stories. Their kids rise up and call them blessed.

Women like my mom who threw off the depression of her upbringing in her twenties by finding the truth that set her free and paving the way for generations of Butler's to find hope and walk in the light. She always held my brother and me and my dad to a higher standard. She put something on the inside of us, that something that made you know when things were not quite right and that you couldn't sleep until you made them right.

Special thanks to Liza and Louisa who approached me about doing a book like this a year ago. Their interest and ideas helped me realize it was time and it prompted me to make it happen.

Every one of these Powerful Female Immigrants has a story to share, and it's not just their story that is so compelling but it's what they did when faced with insurmountable odds.

Read their stories, get to know them, follow them on social media and reach out to them. They truly want to help people take action and go to the next level.

I've been able to get to know many of these wonderful ladies personally over the past few years and see them be a blessing to so many in business and in life. We've since gotten together several times and the amazing synergy continues to grow as these amazing women get to know one another, collaborate and plan further ventures together.

Six years ago I learned of a work in the nation of Pakistan that was feeding fifty orphaned children in a safe house. After months of conversations with the team on the ground I decided to make a trip there. When I saw the need and learned the level of care they were providing for these kids not only physically but also mentally and spiritually it made sense for me to start a nonprofit so we could help even more and 1040Impact.org was founded.

Many trips later and taking our board members to see the work firsthand, including two of our authors who let a women's conference, we've been able to expand the work there to rescue dozens more kids, many who had been trafficked and others who had been orphaned or were working as slaves in the brink kiln factory from ages 4-15.

After the US and allied troops pulled out of Afghanistan parents were so desperate they sold their young daughters to traffickers. We were able to intercept, rescue and save many of these girls and the number of children we are now feeding, clothing, educating and ministering to in our safe house and school has grown to 328. We have a full-time team and dedicated staff, many of whom were orphaned themselves are "paying it forward' in their service to help raise and educate a new generation of young people who are self-sufficient and will never be trafficked or slaves again. Our job skills program is helping the young women gain skills in cosmetology and others industries to prepare them for life beyond high school.

One hundred percent of the proceeds from the sale of Powerful Female Immigrants will go to help fund the ongoing work of 1040Impact.org. Your gifts are tax-deductible and can be made online.

Michael D. Butler, CEO
BeyondPublishing.net
Founder 1040Impact.org

BUSY BODY AND CURIOUS SOUL

Kerry Yu, China

I had just returned from the Miss Universe pageant, where my client had completed a week's worth of grueling competition, testing her on her preparation, skills, and mental toughness at every level. Pushing her mind and being to the limits for the Miss Universe title. I was proud of the work she had put into this moment. This was the path she had chosen, and I was a part of that, helping her compete and win on that stage.

"Kerry is the best mentor anyone could ever dream of having. She has helped me to be who I am today. I am grateful to have her as my manager. I hope her knowledge and experiences will help more people."

Miss Universe Canada 2022
Amelia Tu

For nearly three decades, I have been part of the modeling, fashion, and beauty industry, assisting individuals in realizing their aspiration and objectives. Whether in New York, Milan, or Los

Angeles, the industry has always been characterized by the same desires, dreams, and goals that people set for themselves. Witnessing the miraculous transformation of a young woman stepping into her greatness, discovering her inner lioness, and confidently embracing the present and future she has worked her entire life to prepare for has been an extraordinary experience for me as a coach, mentor, and consultant.

I was once that young girl, growing up wide-eyed and optimistic in China. I recall holding that round globe in my hand for the first time in second grade, memorizing the countries of the world and their locations over the oceans. As I spun the globe in my hand, I could envision all the people from every nation, dreaming, traveling, conversing, and laughing together as one.

I imagined what it would be like in those countries, what the people who lived there were thinking, feeling, and dreaming at that very moment. Were they similar to me? How were they different? Could we become friends and share the stage? Who would be watching?

Finding My Independence at an Early Age

I was fortunate to be raised by parents who let me discover my independence early. They encouraged discovery and exploration, so my brother and I would understand the consequences and rewards of our choices early.

My family sometimes allowed me to figure out things on my own. They didn't make all my decisions for me. I always felt that my parents were smart and brave. When I look back to 70s and 80s, we were fortunate because my parents had good jobs. One thing our family used to do was to have family meetings after dinner. We would sit together, play cards, and then talk about ideas and the future. Those were the best times of my life.

My Love for Travel and How it Shaped My Life

Growing up, my parents believed that education was crucial and provided us with many opportunities to travel around China. From a young age, I was exposed to different cultures and histories, and I soaked it all up like a sponge. These trips were my crash course in education and helped shape my love for travel.

Like many Asian parents, my parents placed a strong emphasis on education for my brother and me. Education provided us choices. I obtained my bachelor's degree at the age of 21 in China before heading to Canada to pursue my passion in the fashion and design industry.

Leaving China for Canada

Leaving China was not a hard time for me; it was a rite of passage where I opened the door to new possibilities. Through my independence, I was able to discover my own identity and how I wanted to relate to the world. Thankfully, my parents were not overly protective, and I was given the chance to learn and grow.

Starting Companies, My Key to Success

I realized early in life that I had a knack for business. I could start a company, create products, find customers, sell those products, and take re-orders before most of my classmates could make it across the street.

The world is a stage, and we are merely actors. From the beginning, I chose to write my own plot, giving me control of the scene and ensuring the outcome of the play. Early on, I found my passion in the business world, and I discovered that it could fuel my dream of creating stages for people all around the globe.

Finding the Right Partners

Finding the right friends, business partners, or soulmate requires wisdom, intuition, and people skills. Although I have not always chosen wisely, I have learned from my mistakes and have always landed on my feet. Having a big picture strategy and balanced expectations can help when making relationship decisions.

Money is Just a Tool

Money is important, but it is only a tool. As a fashion model and a general manager of my company earning a six-figure income at a young age, I have learned that money cannot buy happiness or provide true peace of mind.

My Favorite Job is Being a Mom

Shakespeare said it best: *"All the world's a stage."* I have achieved a great deal, tasting the success of business and financial gain. However, I have come to realize that money is merely a tool and not my purpose. I choose freedom over comfort and value the spotlight but also know when to step away from it. As we progress through different stages of life, we play various roles— sometimes as the main character and sometimes in supporting roles. Regardless of the part I am given, I strive to perform it well.

When my two children were young, I devoted my life to being a stay-at-home mom because my success was not measured by how much money I could make or what kind of material possessions I could acquire. It was measured by what kind of children I could bring into this world. At the end of the day, I believe that there is a difference between what kind of children you could leave to this world and what kind of world you could leave for the children.

Finally Breaking Up

After years of attempting to salvage my marriage, I ultimately concluded that it was in the best interest of both my children's emotional well-being and my own to pursue a divorce. As a result, when my children were aged 10 and 12, I became a single mother with no relatives residing in the United States, no familial support, and no child support payments. Nevertheless, I proudly raised my two children on my own, living in an upscale neighborhood and attending one of the best schools in the state. Rather than viewing myself as a victim, I always believed that everything happens for a reason and was willing to challenge myself to achieve the best possible outcome. I approached this difficult moment in my life with the mindset of "When life gives you lemons, make lemonade." Rather than dwelling on negative emotions, my focus was on finding solutions and improving the situation. In this regard, I find Nike's slogan, "Just do it," particularly inspiring.

The truth is, I'm not a victim; you are not a victim. People who stay stuck in victim mode really don't want success; they just want sympathy. I decided long ago I could settle for sympathy, or I could claim success as my birthright, and I'll take success every time!

Building Character – Finding Courage

Ten years have passed since I was a single mother, and now my children have grown into amazing individuals. My daughter, who is 22 years old, is currently pursuing her graduate studies in psychology. Along with her studies, she also holds two jobs, one as an administrator in her school and the other in a non-profit organization that supports women in need. My son, who is 20 years old, is a talented D1 college football player.

As a parent, I have always strived to be a positive influence on my children. I have taught them to be responsible individuals with a strong sense of purpose towards society. My parents were my role models, and I have become the same for my children.

Now that my children are grown up, I have more free time for myself.. I continue to pursue my passion as a producer and creative director for my shows. I work with fashion designers, models, and I even train pageant girls like Miss Universe Canada Amelia Tu. I have 4 LLCs and a nonprofit,and I love to keep myself busy. I stay curious because that is the secret to staying young.

I firmly believe that life is what you make of it. We should always strive to be happy and take on challenges along the way. Happiness is a state of mind, and it is a choice. We should not be afraid of the unknown, nor of change. Let's embrace life and make the most of every moment.

Creating Influence

I have spent a million or two dollars on plane tickets. I feel like I still have my childhood globe in my hand and that if I fly fast enough, the sun will never set.

Every day, I'm challenged by my children, my students, and my clients to remember that influence isn't measured by the size of your bank account. It is measured by how many lives you touch, how many hearts you inspire, and how many positive changes you create.

So, I urge you to create your own stage, a platform that will endure and make a difference. You probably already know what you stage is. Don't envy someone else's spotlight, embrace your own, nurture it, and let it grow. Invite others to join you, share their talents, and learn from their mistakes. Stages are not meant to be exclusive, but, rather, to be shared, passed on, and amplified. Don't live small; live big, with all your gifts and creativity, and shine a light on others so they can shine, too.

As for me, I'll always be a busy body and a curious soul, with a hunger for new experiences and a thirst for learning.

Kerry Yu

With nearly 30 years of fashion experience as an international model and fashion show producer, Kerry Yu is a seasoned expert in her field.

In the 1990s, she earned numerous modeling awards in Canadian modeling competitions. Since then, she has produced fashion shows and events for over a hundred designers and brands across the globe, including New York Fashion Week, Vancouver Fashion Week, Toronto Fashion

Week, Dubai Fashion Week, China Fashion Week, and China U.S. Fashion Week .

Kerry Yu is the founder of China U.S. Fashion Week and a director of International Modeling and Talent Association in U.S. She manages Miss Universe Canada Amelia Tu, serves as the fashion editor of *Lake Oswego Life/ Style* Magazine and is the CEO of Oceana Blue Productions, LLC.

Currently residing in Oregon, Kerry Yu's expertise and leadership have left an indelible mark on the fashion industry, and she continues to inspire and empower emerging talent around the world.

Kerry Yu can be reached for media, speaking, and interviews at
OceanaBlueUSA.com and *PowerfulFemaleImmigrants.com*

THE DECLARATION OF INDEPENDENCE OF A NIGERIAN LIONESS!

Dr. Olayinka Holt, MD, Nigeria

Rising through the obstacles of a male-dominated world to become who I am today as an independent successful physician, single mother, real estate investor, and entrepreneur has been my unique journey.

My name is Dr. Olayinka Holt. Olayinka means "I'm surrounded by wealth." While this was true when I was born, there were times when I experienced periods of extreme poverty growing up. My dad was an extremely smart man. He dropped out of high school because his grandmother and sponsor died. Unfortunately, his mother was unable to continue paying the tuition. However, he studied at home and challenged the WASC examination, passed, and began working as a salesman. My father also self-taught himself civil engineering. He passed the exam and began working as a building contractor.

I knew my dad to be very hard working. He started his own business. When I was about eight years old, my dad would ask me to balance his books. I did very well with book-keeping and balancing his books. He made me a signatory to his business accounts. My dad would always tell us that hard work is the foundation of success.

I was fortunate to be smart, and I went through elementary school and high school with a breeze. I was also able to get into college at a very young age and graduated before I was 19 years old. I lived in extreme poverty most of these years. I wore old dresses in college, I had few toiletries, and little to no cash. But that didn't stop my strong belief to become someone in life. I was able to obtain a master's degree in organic chemistry, and also pursued a PhD in organic chemistry. While undergoing my PhD degree, I met a man whom I thought was the love of my life. Unfortunately, life can be hard and painful, and the man that I thought was the love of my life turned out to be a womanizer. He chased everything in a skirt. I decided to be blind to everything he was doing because I had been brainwashed that a woman, I had to endure whatever happened in my marriage! I was also made to believe it's an abomination to divorce. Because of the situation, I began planning my escape. I told my husband that I would love to have my children in the United States. I thought they would be U.S. citizens, and it would be easy for us to leave when the time was right. Just as I imagined, it all began after I came to the United States to have my daughter. I came back home six months after having my daughter in Chicago. I waited at the airport for so many hours, but my husband did not show up to pick me up. I took a taxi from the international airport, which is about an hour drive to my home. As I was getting to my home, my husband was returning from church with his girlfriend. My heart sank within me. I felt my world crumbling at my feet! This was something I had decided to be blind to, and was then hitting me in the face.

My husband told me that I had a choice to either stay or go away, but he was not going to leave that woman for me. I struggled to believe that I could build a life with this man. I wanted to believe that there was something good for me in this life with him. I thought my happiness was to be in a marriage with children, living in a big house, and having good friends! Unfortunately, none of that was bringing me happiness. None of his fame, wealth, and charisma were sufficient for my happiness. What's worse was that he kept his word. He never sent the woman away. I had to stay in the house with the woman for three months.

I became the laughingstock of neighbors. The three months I stayed in the house felt like being in prison for 30 years in my own home. It felt as if I was in a dream, a terrible nightmare that I prayed to wake up from. I found myself in a pool of dark waters. I went into deep depression. I would wake up in the morning and cry my eyes out. I resolved to drink alcohol and smoke cigarettes, and just prayed that things would change. I knew something had to change. I remember my core beliefs. I knew what I had to do, and I prayed that God would give me the strength to find myself and the courage to do the things that I was about to embark upon.

I knew I had to step out of that dark life to live an everlasting life of peace, comfort, and purpose. I recall seeking advice from some aunts and aunts-in-law on how they were able to sustain their marriage and live a peaceful life. Unknown to me, everyone buried their feelings. I was told by my great aunt that she had to fetch water for her husband's concubine after they finish "the act," and she pleaded with me to endure whatever I was going through with my husband. When I was going through the depression and anxiety, one morning, my husband came to my room. I opened the door and he said to me, "Look at you. You're a caricature of yourself; you don't even look beautiful anymore.

How could you allow yourself to be like this? I think your best bet is to return to America and make a life for yourself". He also said, "I heard that if you enroll and complete a course in nursing, your employer will file for a 'green card.' After that, you can start working as a nurse, send your money back home, and I can help you to invest the money."

I remember saying to myself, *How can I ever trust this guy who I gave my heart and life to, and he betrayed my love? Is this all about money or slavery? Does this man think I would be dumb enough to send my earnings to him to be with other women?* All sorts of thoughts were going through my mind. I could not believe what I was experiencing.

I prayed to God to give me the strength to find myself. I asked him to give me the courage to step out of this situation and become the woman He created me to be. I knew the change was inevitable and that I was about to go through proverbial hell. I finally summoned my courage, spoke to my dad, narrated the ordeals, and informed him of my plan to leave my husband. Unfortunately, his response was even more disheartening! Much as my dad respected me and always encouraged me to excel in life and be a strong woman, the fact that he was a traditional chief clouded his judgement. He told me I would be the black sheep of the family if I decided to divorce my husband. No woman in their family has ever divorced their husband. However, I was determined to leave him. I was prepared to make the change, even though it meant I would need to walk a lot of miles alone until I could find others who would walk the same path with me and help me find my voice.

I returned to the United States with so much determination. My desire to change my situation was unstoppable. I needed to show myself and the whole world that I can survive without being married.

I needed to prove myself that I could leave and make a change in the world without having to go through the emotional and physical abuse that women go through for the sake of marriage.

I recalled one of my aunts advised me to make sure to have a second child, just so that if I decided not to be married again, I would have two children and not have to be worried about having any more children. The advice did not make sense to me at the time, but I went ahead with it. I decided to have a second child. I had my second child in New York. I was overwhelmed with joy. I named him "Oluwadamilare," meaning the Lord has vindicated me.

I decided not to return to Nigeria although my visa was a business class. I was determined to make a new life for myself and my two children alone.

About a month after my son was born, I got a call from my husband that he was coming to visit me. He was going to stop by the United Kingdom for three days and then, he would come to the United States. For the three days he was in the U.K., he would not give me his contact phone number because he was visiting another woman who also just had a baby for him.

When he arrived, I asked about his whereabouts in the U.K. He could not tell me anything. He would go out to make phone calls to talk to the woman, so I would not find out.

On the third day of his visit when he came back from making the phone call, I went in the closet and threw all his clothes in his suitcase. I put the suitcase outside. I poured myself a glass of scotch on the rocks and declared my independence. I told him it was over between us and that I was determined to make it with or without him. That night, I felt I finally stepped into my power. I felt free and relieved.

It was a very hard journey and rocky road. I found myself working all sorts of small jobs. I saved some money, which was used for evaluating my transcript from Nigeria. I was able to start teaching. I registered to be a substitute teacher. I taught chemistry, physics, biology, and general science to high school students in the New York metropolis. I also worked as a child protective specialist with the Administration for Children's Services (ACS), investigating all cases of child abuse and neglect, and helping protect children who were born into drug-infested homes and emotionally abused children.

While going through this job, I thought I had found my calling. I felt so much love in my heart for the Universe. I wanted to help everyone that I could touch. I helped every life that came through my path. I believed that I was wonderfully and beautifully made by God to help humanity. I found myself wanting more.

While trying to settle myself in the U.S.A., l received the sad news that one of my sisters had died while giving birth to her second child. I was overwhelmed with grief, especially after finding out that she developed kidney failure. She underwent hemodialysis briefly and died. The desire to become a physician burned through me. I decided to pursue my long-term career ambition. I had always wanted to pursue a medical career. That was possible for me in Nigeria. It was one of my goals that once I got to America, the land of opportunities, I would become a doctor.

In 2000, I was returning home from work one day when I drove past the State University of New York (SUNY) in Farmingdale. I stopped by and inquired about the medicine program. I was handed a bucket list of requirements. I went through the list. I took a course for over nine months. I was accepted into medical school in Belize, Central America, and started in September 2001.

I studied medicine in Belize. I did not know anyone in that country. I learned that when you are determined, you become blinded to obstacles. My favorite scripture verse is:

"I can do all things through Christ who strengthens me"
Phillippians 4:13.

I also learned to put my trust in God in all my undertakings, and He has never failed me. My other favorite scripture verse is in Proverbs 3, 5-6:

"Trust in the Lord with all thine heart;
And lean not unto thine own understanding.
In all thy ways, acknowledge Him,
and He shall direct thy paths."

As an immigrant woman in the U.S.A., a unique set of challenges and obstacles are encountered, such as having to navigate issues related to gender, race, and nationality. Despite these challenges, immigrant women such as myself have made significant contributions to American society and have achieved success in a variety of fields. However, the journey to success is not always easy, and it's important to recognize and address the barriers that immigrant women face in order to create a more equitable society. According to the Migration Policy Institute, there were 21.5 million immigrant women living in the United States in 2019, making up nearly 52 percent of the immigrant population.

It is my courage I now give you.

I give you power, the tools you need to reach your extraordinary potential. Finding your voice, women, a voice to make decisions that affect your life and the lives of those around you.

I give you a community, where we promote gender equality, end discrimination, and create a world where women are valued and respected.

I give you a heartbeat. Women need role models and examples to look up to. Women who have succeeded in fields traditionally dominated by men, who have overcome adversity, and who have broken through barriers to achieve their goals. Women who inspire other women, who can show other women what is possible, and encourage them to aim high and pursue their dreams.

I give you self-awareness, which is crucial to women's empowerment. Women must be able to recognize and challenge the internalized biases and societal expectations that may hold them back. Critical self-awareness involves examining our beliefs, thoughts, and actions and questioning where they come from and how they affect us. By becoming more self-aware, you can identify your strengths, set realistic goals, and develop the confidence and resilience you need to overcome obstacles.

You are not the first to find your voice. I celebrate others who have come before us.

Malala Yousafzai - Malala is a Pakistani activist for girls' education who was shot by the Taliban in 2012 for her advocacy work. She survived the attack and went on to become the youngest Nobel Prize laureate, continuing her work to ensure all girls have access to education.

Marie Curie - Marie Curie was a Polish-born physicist and chemist who conducted pioneering research on radioactivity. She was the first woman to win a Nobel Prize, and the first person ever to win two Nobel Prizes in different fields.

Kamala Harris - Kamala Harris is the first woman, first Black woman, and first Asian-American woman to serve as Vice President of the United States. She has broken through barriers in politics and continues to inspire young women and girls to pursue their dreams.

Oprah Winfrey - Oprah Winfrey is a media mogul, philanthropist, and actress who overcame a difficult childhood to become one of the most successful and influential women in the world. She has used her platform to promote education, health, and social justice issues.

Ada Lovelace - Ada Lovelace was a British mathematician and writer who is credited with creating the first computer program, long before the invention of modern computers. She broke through barriers in the male-dominated field of science and technology, and her work continues to inspire generations of women in STEM.

Now it's our turn.
Impossible to love you more.
Yinka

For more information and to receive free e-books on real estate investing, visit me at: *www.promeritinvestments.com*

Dr. Olayinka Holt, MD

Dr. Olayinka Holt is an accredited investor and the Principal of ProMerit Investments LLC, a private equity firm. She is a single mother of three children; number 9 of 13 children from her father. She relocated to the U.S.A. in 1992 after completing her elementary school through university education in Ibadan, Oyo State Nigeria. At age 16, she got admission to the University of Ibadan where she majored in chemistry and minored in zoology; graduating with her bachelor's degree at the young age of 19. She is a board-certified physician and sole proprietor of a successful medical clinic. Since 2012 she has been serving the South Texas community, which she is very passionate about. Her mission is to inspire and empower migrant women across the US to courageously follow their dreams. In her spare time, she enjoys watching movies, cooking, and taking scenic drives with her children.

Dr. Olayinka can be reach at:
promeritinvestments.com & PowerfulFemaleImmigrants.com

THE LIONHEARTED WOMAN

Barbara Heil-Sonneck, Germany

In every situation we encounter in our lives, we have the choice of how we perceive and how we react to it. There is always something to learn from it. Our mind is an amazing vehicle. There is a quote from Henry Ford that I have always taken to heart, "Whether you think you can or you think you can't, you're right." Since my childhood, I looked at the glass half full and never let negative thoughts and energy derail me. I have made plenty of mistakes on my journey, however, they all have been steppingstones on my journey of life. And I will share some here, as well as my successes.

I am v Heil-Sonneck, a heart-centered leader with a positive mindset.

Speak the truth with honesty.

Pause and think before you speak.

Lead with your heart and empathy.

Always act with integrity…

Both of my parents' families are from the "Sudetenland" former Czechoslovakia, now the Czech Republic and Slovakia after the peaceful separation in 1993. Both my mother and father's families had left that area and settled in Germany after World War II.

My Mom

After WWII, at 12 years old, her family lost everything; their home, land, and belongings. My mom always shared vividly how she experienced the moment when she was told to leave everything behind. She hid her little treasures under an old oak tree in the garden. They all rushed to pack a few clothes and food, then everyone started running. There had been five women and my grandfather running the farm. My mom, her mom, my mom's sister, my cousin, myself, and my grandfather. My cousin's father had died early in the war.

My mom never knew her father. We only learned later that her mom was raped by the owner of a mill she was working for. But at that time, it was always somehow the girl's fault.

They were running for their lives. The Russians were coming, and as we know, war does not paint a pretty picture, no matter where in the world and from whom you are running.

For days, they walked and hid in the cornfields until they arrived at a safe place. The five women found a room to share in a small village in Bavaria.

At 16, Mom left for Wuerzburg and found a bakery. She ran the household for the owners, cooked, and helped to raise the owner's two sons. She also helped in the little shop when needed. After I was born, she took a break then worked part time until she left. The owners had to hire three people to replace her.

My Dad

There were five children in my father's family. Grandpa was originally very supportive of the regime during the war. He was a recipient of the Iron Cross medal. After he learned what was really happening, he spoke out. As a result, he was sent to the front to be part of a "Death Squad," where he died.

When the Lieutenant of his squad delivered the sad new to my grandma, she threw them out and pulled the pictures of Goebbels and Hitler that they were required to display from the wall. She shouted, "Take the letter and these murderers with you, they have no place here." She spoke her truth and was lucky that the lieutenant was a family friend. Grandma was very strong; she was part of the "Truemmer Frauen or Rubble Women" who after the war, helped clear and reconstruct the bombed cities. With so many men dead or prisoners of war, this monumental task fell mostly on women.

I share these stories to provide some insights into what my parents' families experienced, what they stood for, and their core values. It explains how I was raised.

My parents met in my hometown, Wuerzburg, a beautiful university city on the River Main, in the northern part of Bavaria. They married and rented a tiny Studio. We had a modest life without even a TV until I was 6 or 7 and spent a lot of time outdoors. Dad was always an artist at heart, painting or writing poems and stories. But he had to take a job to support first his mom and siblings and later his family. Mom worked part time and took care of me. Dad was the strong family patriarch, and he always encouraged and supported finding time to breathe, listen to classical music, rest, and spend time with family and friends. Mom was driven to create a better life and for me to study and get out. I believe the determination and drive I have is inherited from her.

Love Who You Are and Never Stop Growing

I was a very quiet and shy child. I typically disappeared in the crowd, which was not easy, since I was so tall. Once, I was even mistaken for the teacher. I was more of a tomboy, playing soccer, running around, and active with short hair. I didn't get much attention. I liked being part of the crowd, not the leader. I was comfortable not being noticed, until I finally learned that I could be just as comfortable letting my voice be heard.

A Special Event

I was in third grade at school during a break. Two boys were snapping me with a rubber band. I asked them to stop two or three times. I can't remember what came over me. I acted on instinct. I quickly turned, raised my arms, and tossed the two boys' heads together. That stopped my torture. I know what I did was not right, and I should have reported it to the teacher. However, when I did, I was the one who had to stand in the corner of the classroom, not all three of us. I didn't feel like I was fairly treated.

I decided to go on strike by not participating in class. I felt I deserved an apology for how I was treated by the teacher. I don't recall if my teacher apologized, but this was a major breakthrough in my life. I no longer felt like a victim, and I was now able to walk tall, to stand up for my beliefs, and to overcome my fears of being put on the spot.

From this moment on, I started to love taking responsibility. I was selected as the speaker of the class the following year and through high school.

Losing a Parent

Until I was 11, there were lot of beautiful childhood memories and loving times with my parents and family in that one-bedroom apartment. We spent most of our vacations at my two aunts' little farm, where my mom was raised after the war. The farmhouse was small. There was an outhouse and a pee pan under the bed. For warmth, we had to build a fire in the oven. We slaughtered and harvested. When the baker visited once a week in his van, it was always a highlight for us.

After returning from the farm that year, my dad took me on a walk and shared that my mom had cancer and only had a short time left. My little world broke apart. Mom was a fighter and mostly upbeat until her last day. I was the one holding on to hope and did not want to let her go. She passed a year later. I chose to take care of us, cooking, doing the household chores, and doing some shopping.

My dad was lost, devastated, and he started to drink more than was good for him. I found it was better to stay away from him.

Two years later, dad met a wonderful woman, who had two kids, and we became a patchwork family. My new mom was a blessing, and I suddenly gained an older sister und younger brother. Life started to look sunny again.

I left home at 18. The two years before that had been quite a struggle, and my dad's alcohol intake had increased. We learned to tiptoe around the vibes to keep the peace in the house. There were good days and bad days. When I left, I went right into an abusive relationship with a man twice my age. It was not physically abusive, but it was psychologically and economically abusive. At first, I did not even recognize it. This man was highly intelligent and caring, at least I thought so, at first. Step by step, I entered the web of his intrigues and schemes.

After a year-and-a-half, I finally was strong enough to leave at night with only what I was wearing and knowing that I also had a long legal fight ahead, since I co-signed some business papers on a part ownership of his company. At 19 years old, I was facing a huge debt and a new start. I learned a lot of legal process and negotiation.

Biggest lesson learned: Don't let your pride and or fear prevent you from leaving or saying **no**.

Test-Driving – Off to a New Start in My Career

I loved marketing, and I landed a position with the #1 publishing house for computer magazines and books in Germany. I became a junior marketing specialist, then assistant manager, all while completing my bachelor's degree in marketing in evening classes.

After five years in advertising, I met my first husband, and we moved to Frankfurt. I began working as an operations manager for DELL Computer. I even got to meet Michael Dell at my first meeting. I was then given an opportunity to manage an IBM call center organization then lead other projects in Europe.

My first marriage ended. We parted ways, no big drama.

Visualization is Key, Painting a Picture of My Next Goal.

I had a dream to work in a foreign country. Shortly after I told my general manager, I was selected for an opportunity and moved to the United States in 1996. I then held several management positions in global sales and operations working with teams all over the world until June 2005.

Starting My Real Estate Venture

In 2001, a friend asked me if I would ever consider investing in real estate, and I answered **yes**. We got a solid basic education and looked at at least 100 houses before we finally bought our first home for renovation. During that first remodel, we made a common "starter" mistake and went **cheap** on our contractors. We ended up doing a lot of work by ourselves, from installing laminate, finishing Sheetrock, redoing hardware, and so on….

We learned a lot, finished the deal, rented for a year, and sold with a total of a net $30K profit.

During this time, I met my soulmate, my second husband. You really have to love someone if you still kiss your girlfriend when she looks like a snowman covered in Sheetrock dust.

Big Lesson: Cheap Will Cost You

We continued our real estate quest. After the first experience, it was important to have a good crew of contractors, which is key for every successful remodel. And the key focuses during the remodel have been ROI (return on investment), design features, and staging.

In 2003, my son was born, and oh, life changed. I cut back on travel, accepted a part-time position, continued investing, holding, and flipping. I grew a nice portfolio of several rentals, most of them in partnerships, with shared responsibilities and the flexibility I was seeking.

Starting a Second Business

In 2005, I ended my corporate career, focusing my time on real estate investing and coaching.

I discovered I got the most satisfaction in the creative process from design and staging. After years of corporate, I was yearning for a hands-on approach and control in my hands. The new idea of Design2Sell was born in the Fall of 2006, and the new company was founded shortly after.

Sixteen years later, Design2Sell is a thriving staging company, serving the metro Atlanta market. We developed a proven system that will result in measurable and marketable results and the highest ROI (return on investment) for our clients. We have been called the "secret weapon" and "the closer" on many deals. Our team has won top industry awards year after year. I am so proud how our team is running the operation with minimal involvement from my side.

Biggest Lesson Learned: If you want to grow, you have to let go.

Starting a Third Business: Back to Brick and Mortar - Multifamily

Values I was raised by: Work hard. Invest in your education. Money does not grow on trees. Be modest. Serve others. Take time for your family. Don't stick out too much from the crowd. Don't waste anything.

Mom and Dad lived a solid but modest life, they created a family culture of hard work and support. My dad's legacy has been his poems and stories, something I truly treasure. But money was always just enough. When Dad left this earth, there was nothing left for Mom to fall back on.

Those things never came easy, but I was always reaching for the next goal, looking at every situation as a lesson and opportunity to better myself. In the past five years, I was feeling stuck in the day-to-day of the business and life, and I stopped listening to **me**.

Two years ago, I attended a Grant Cardone event, and that started a big mindshift transition in my life. I asked myself some serious questions about my business. I started to explore and educate myself more. The 10X Mindset made me look at everything differently. I then listened to Ed Mylett's speech "The Power of One More," and that was the strategy I could embrace and live by which would eventually lead to 10X thinking.

In the last 10 months, I invested in three limited partnership deals, converted from a business owner to shareholder mindset, started a local multifamily networking group, and I am actively looking for warehouse space to buy, preparing another single-family home investment for sale, and will invest the proceeds into an apartment building and continue to invest into other businesses. Everything is possible!

Every year, I look for new challenges that will help me learn something new, stay sharp, and stay humble. It challenges me to always be a beginner. Some examples of my challenges include taking singing lessons, writing a book, scuba diving, snowshoe trips, painting, diving with the sharks, and hiking Manchu Picchu.

People sometimes ask me how I find time for all these activities. My answer is **love**!

I love what I do, and I always look for ways to grow. And if you love something, you will find and make time for it.

Back in 2007, when I co-authored my first book, I dove deeper into the "Venus Approach to Doing Business." The Venus Approach was created to **connect** the readers with other highly successful women in their field. To offer a positive and motivating forum to **share, experience, and learn**, as well as to provide women with plenty of comprehensive resources, some of which cannot be found anywhere else. It still took me 15 years to finally discover the bigger picture of multifamily.

It's no longer a secret that women think, act, and communicate differently. We also have a distinct way of doing business. Women use their own innately female skills, which may not be as aggressive but can be equally competitive conducting business.

Statistics show that women live longer than men, and at the same time, they often get paid less in their jobs. Life's circumstances lead many women to contribute fewer years toward their Social Security and pension benefits. Financial experts urge women to save and invest more to create a solid asset portfolio to secure a comfortable lifestyle during their later years.

Barbara Heil-Sonneck

Through my experiences, I have learned how to find opportunities that give me financial independence and long-term stability.

My vision is to help successful, mature women to leverage their immense experience and success by harnessing the power of investments and partnerships, so they can move beyond the limitations of entrepreneurship to achieve more passive income while having a massive impact. My mission is to help as many women as I can with that journey.

The charity of my choice, SAPREA, liberates individuals and society from child sexual abuse and its lasting impacts.

"Breaking Boundaries, Building Bridges:
Strategies for Success as a Female Immigrant"

Barbara can be reach at:
instagram.com/barbaraheilsonneck
PowerfulFemaleImmigrants.com

THE GOLDEN CAGE: A SHELTERED LIFE OF LUXURY AND CULTURE

Dr. Dalal Akoury, Egypt

I was born into a world of privilege, where maids, cooks, and butlers were a normal part of my daily life. My father was a prominent Civil engineer and the minister of transportation in Egypt, my mother was a successful real-estate owner and investor. My parents built their wealth through hard work and determination, and they were determined to give their children every advantage in life.

Growing up in this sheltered world, I was shielded from many of the harsh realities that others faced. I went to private Catholic schools of French nuns, took music and dance lessons, and spent summers traveling with my family. We lived in a spacious home on the Mediterranean Sea with a large garden, where I spent many afternoons playing with my siblings and enjoying the sunshine. My family was of Egyptian descent, and we lived amid a community that was proud of its heritage. I grew up hearing Arabic, and French spoken at home and at community events, and I learned to appreciate the richness of Lebanese culture.

While I loved this comfortable life, I was aware that it was not the norm for everyone. As I grew older and began to interact with people from different backgrounds, I realized that my upbringing was a privilege that not everyone shared.

Despite the comfort and luxury of my upbringing, I was never content to rest on my laurels. From an early age, I was driven to succeed and make a difference in the world. I had a passion for learning and a thirst for knowledge that could not be quenched. And although my sheltered life had shielded me from many of the harsh realities of the world, I was keenly aware of the challenges that lay ahead.

Looking back, I realize that my upbringing gave me a unique perspective on life. I was privileged in many ways, but I was also acutely aware of the responsibilities that came with that privilege. I learned to appreciate the value of hard work and perseverance, and I was determined to make the most of the opportunities that came my way.

As I look back on my life, I am grateful for the sheltered upbringing that gave me a strong foundation for success. But I am also aware that there were many challenges and obstacles that lay ahead. In the paragraphs that follow, I will share the story of my journey, the struggles and triumphs, and the lessons that I have learned along the way.

The Loss That Changed Everything: Overcoming Tragedy and Finding Purpose

When I was 17 years old, my father who was the rock of our family passed away from pancreatic cancer. His passing created a void that could never be filled. It was a devastating blow for me and my family, and it changed the course of my life forever. For me, the loss of my father was very difficult. He was my role model and my inspiration. I always looked up to him as a source of guidance and support. His death left a gaping hole in my life that I struggled to fill.

My father a successful businessman, was a heavy smoker and coffee drinker, and he lived with constant stress. It was a lethal combination that ultimately led to his untimely death. In the wake of his passing, my family was left in shock and grief.

For me, the loss of my father was especially difficult. Nonetheless in the midst of my grief, I realized that I had a choice. I could succumb to the pain and give up on my dreams, or I could use the experience as a catalyst for change. I chose the latter. I made the decision to beat cancer, to pursue a medical career that would allow me to help others, and to make a difference in the world.

It was not an easy path. I faced many obstacles and challenges along the way. But I was determined to succeed, to honor my father's memory, and to make a difference in the world.

Looking back, I realize that my father's death was a turning point in my life. It was a wake-up call that reminded me of the fragility of life and the importance of making the most of the time we have.

In the paragraphs that follow, I will share the story of my journey, the struggles and triumphs, and the lessons that I have learned along the way.

Choosing to Beat Cancer:
My Journey to Medical School and Beyond

After my father's death, I knew that I had to do something to honor his memory and to make a difference in the world. I decided to pursue a career in medicine, with the goal of helping others overcome the same challenges that my father faced.

It was not an easy path. As a female immigrant, I faced many obstacles and challenges along the way. But I was determined to succeed, and I was willing to make sacrifices to make my dreams a reality. Of course, when I made the decision to pursue a career in medicine after my father's death, I knew that I was taking on a monumental challenge. I was not only a woman in a field that was dominated by men, but I was also a foreigner in a new country, with a different language and culture to navigate. I was determined to succeed, no matter what obstacles lay in my path. I threw myself into my studies with a fierce determination, working long hours and sacrificing my social life to achieve my goals.

There were times when I was tempted to give up, when the challenges seemed insurmountable and the sacrifices too great. But I kept pushing forward, driven by the memory of my father and the desire to make a difference in the world.

Over time, my hard work and determination paid off. I excelled in my studies and received the support and mentorship of those who recognized my talent and potential. I began to see that my dreams were within reach, and that I had the ability to make a meaningful contribution to the world.

Looking back on those years, I realize that I learned some valuable lessons along the way. I learned the importance of perseverance, of never giving up on your dreams, no matter how daunting the challenges may seem. I learned that success requires hard work and sacrifice, but that the rewards are well worth the effort.

In the paragraphs that follow, I will share the story of my journey, the struggles and triumphs, and the lessons that I have learned along the way.

Stranger in a Strange Land Breaking Barriers:
My Journey as a Female Foreigner in the Medical Field

After completing my medical studies and training in Egypt, I made the decision to move to the United States to pursue my career as a physician. But as a female immigrant in a new country, I faced many challenges that I had not anticipated.

One of the biggest challenges I faced was the language barrier. Although I was fluent in English, I had to adjust to a new dialect and colloquialisms that were unfamiliar to me. I also had to navigate the complex cultural differences between Egypt and the United States, learning to adapt to a new way of life and work.

As a foreign-trained physician, I also faced challenges in the medical profession. I had to prove myself to colleagues and patients alike, demonstrating my expertise and knowledge in a new environment. I also had to navigate the complexities of the American healthcare system, which was very different from what I was accustomed to in Egypt. I refused to give up. I knew that I had something to offer, and that I could make a difference in the world if I worked hard enough. So, I threw myself into my work with renewed vigor, determined to prove myself to my colleagues and to make a name for myself in my profession.

Along the way, I discovered that my foreign background could be an asset rather than a liability.

Despite these challenges, I remained determined to succeed. I worked hard to learn the language and to adapt to the new culture. I also sought out mentors and colleagues who could provide guidance and support, helping me to overcome the obstacles that I faced.

Over time, I was able to establish myself as a respected physician in my community. I built a successful practice, earning the trust and admiration of my patients and colleagues. And along the way, I learned some important lessons about resilience, perseverance, and the power of determination.

In the paragraphs that follow, I will share the story of my journey, the struggles and triumphs, and the lessons that I have learned along the way.

A Mother's Sacrifice: The Emotional Journey of Leaving My Children to Pursue My Career and Reuniting with Them

Leaving my children in Egypt with my anesthesiologist husband was one of the hardest decisions I ever had to make. As I looked out the airplane window, my eyes filled with tears as I said goodbye to my two sons in Egypt. One was two years old, and one was less than a year. It wasn't easy leaving them behind, but I had made up my mind; if there was any hope of curing cancer, it lay in America. I knew that pursuing my medical career in the United States would require sacrifices, but I never anticipated the emotional toll it would take on me.

For 1.5 years, I worked tirelessly to build my career and to make a difference in the world. But I missed my family every day, and I longed to be reunited with them.

My dad died from the disease just months before and it broke my heart that he had never been able to receive proper treatment - so here I was on this plane, determined to do whatever I could to make sure other families didn't have to suffer like mine did.

The next year-and-a-half seemed like an eternity away from home and away from my children. Even upon coming back home after such a long time apart, they were scared of me for weeks - which absolutely shattered me inside. But despite everything that happened during my absence, something great did come out of it: both of boys pursued degrees in medicine when they grew older! My oldest son eventually became an ER doctor in Tennessee while his younger brother earned a Doctorate Degree in AI technology!

I thank God every day for giving me the strength and courage necessary to make such a hard decision - even though it meant sacrificing precious moments with them throughout their childhoods. In some way or another, we all fight battles against cancer no matter how big or small, whether it's through research or prayer - together we can find hope for tomorrow's generation.

Looking back on that journey, I realize that it taught me some important lessons about the sacrifices that we make in pursuit of our dreams. It taught me that sometimes the price of success is high, and that we must be willing to pay that price if we want to achieve our goals. But it also taught me that the emotional toll of that sacrifice can be just as high, and that we must be mindful of the impact it has on ourselves and our loved ones.

In the paragraphs that follow, I will share the story of my journey, the struggles and triumphs, and the lessons that I have learned along the way.

Mentoring Across Borders: Empowering Female Immigrants to Achieve Their Dreams"

After many years of hard work and dedication, I am proud to say that I have achieved a great deal in my career. Along the way, I have received numerous awards and accolades for my work in the field of medicine, as well as for my writing.

In total, I have received seven awards for my work in medicine, including recognition for my contributions to cancer research and for my efforts to improve the lives of women in medicine. These awards are a testament to the many long hours and hard work that I have put into my career, and I am proud to have achieved so much.

In addition to my work in medicine, I have also written three books on important topics that are close to my heart. "Do Not Eat the Donuts" is a guide to healthy eating and living, while "Cancer Beyond the Cure" is a comprehensive resource for cancer patients and their families. "Sex Addiction Is Not Just a Guy's Thing" being a groundbreaking book that explores the often-overlooked issue of sex addiction in women.

Through my writing and my work in medicine, I have been able to help countless people around the world. I am passionate about mentoring and empowering women, and I believe that everyone has the potential to achieve great things.

I've been able to raise awareness of important issues and help people find the support and resources they need to live healthier, happier lives.

But my greatest achievement is the work I've done as a mentor and a role model for other women. Through my mentoring programs and workshops, I've been able to help countless women achieve their goals and pursue their dreams. I've seen firsthand the transformative power of mentorship, and I'm proud to be able to give back to my community in this way

In the paragraphs that follow, I will share my experiences and the lessons that I have learned along the way, and I will provide strategies for success that can help other women achieve their dreams. I am committed to making a difference in the world, and I believe that together, we can achieve great things.

Unlocking Potential: Strategies for Success as a Female Immigrant

As a female immigrant who has faced many challenges and overcome many obstacles, I am passionate about helping others achieve their dreams. I believe that every woman has the potential to be successful and to make a difference in the world, no matter where she comes from or what challenges she faces.

Through my work as a physician, a writer, and a mentor, I have developed a set of strategies that can help women unlock their potential and achieve their goals. These strategies include:

1. Setting clear goals: I believe that it's important for women to have a clear vision of what they want to achieve. This means setting specific, measurable, and achievable goals that will guide their actions and motivate them to succeed.

2. Seeking out mentors and role models: I have found that having mentors and role models can be incredibly helpful in achieving success. Mentors can offer guidance, support, and advice, while role models can provide inspiration and motivation.

3. Developing a strong work ethic: Success requires hard work and dedication. I believe that women need to be willing to put in the time and effort needed to achieve their goals, and to be persistent in the face of challenges and setbacks.

4. Building a strong support network: No one can achieve success alone. I believe that women need to surround themselves with supportive friends, family, and colleagues who will encourage them and lift them up when they face obstacles.

5. Embracing diversity and cultural differences: As a female immigrant, I have learned the importance of embracing diversity and cultural differences. I believe that women need to be open-minded and respectful of other cultures, and to use their unique perspectives to make a positive impact in the world.

Through my work as a mentor and a physician, I have seen firsthand the power of these strategies in helping women achieve their dreams. I am passionate about empowering women and helping them unlock their full potential, and I believe that with the right mindset and the right support, anything is possible.

Paying it Forward:
The Power of Giving Back to the Community

As I look back on my journey as a female immigrant, I realize that I have been fortunate to have the support and guidance of many mentors and role models along the way. They helped me to overcome obstacles, stay focused on my goals, and to achieve success in my career and in my personal life.

I also realize that not everyone is as fortunate as I have been. Many women struggle to find the support and guidance they need to achieve their dreams, especially as immigrants in a new country. That's why I have made it my mission to pay it forward, to use my own experiences and knowledge to mentor and empower other women.

Through my work as a physician and as an author, I had the opportunity to reach thousands of women around the world. I have shared my own stories of overcoming adversity and achieving success, and I have provided practical advice and guidance for other women who are on a similar journey.

I have established mentoring programs and support networks for female immigrants and other underrepresented groups. These programs provide a safe and supportive space for women to connect with each other, to share their stories and their struggles, and to receive guidance and support from mentors who have walked the same path.

For me, mentoring and empowering others is not just a way to give back. It is also a way to continue to grow and to learn from others. By working with women from diverse backgrounds and cultures, I can gain new perspectives and insights that help me to be a better physician and a better person.

In the end, the only way to empower the next generation of female immigrants is by sharing my own story and my own experiences. By showing other women that it is possible to overcome obstacles and achieve great things, I hope to inspire and motivate them to pursue their own dreams and goals.

I believe that each of us has the power to make a difference in the world. By sharing our stories, our knowledge, and our talents with others, we can empower those around us to achieve their dreams and to create a brighter future for us all.

In my books and mentoring programs that follow, I will share more stories of mentoring and empowerment, as well as practical tips and strategies for women who are looking to achieve their own dreams.

As I come to the end of my journey as a foreigner, I can't help but feel like Frank Sinatra. I did it my way, singing all the way through the ups and downs, the laughter, and the tears.

And just like Frank, I've learned that life is a journey, and that sometimes you must make up the words as you go along. You must laugh when you want to cry, and cry when you want to laugh. But you also must believe in yourself, and in the power of your dreams.

As a female immigrant, I've faced challenges that I never imagined possible. But I've also discovered a strength and resilience that I never knew I had. And I've been inspired by the incredible women who have walked this path before me, and by those who are just starting out.

So, to all the women out there, no matter where you come from or what your dreams may be, I want to say this: believe in yourself, and never give up. You may not know all the words to the song, but if you keep singing, you'll find your way.

And to those who have supported me along the way, I want to say thank you. Thank you for your laughter, for your tears, and for your unwavering support. Without you, this journey would have been so much harder.

As I close this chapter of my life, I look forward to the next adventure. I don't know where it will take me, but I know that with a sense of humor, a lot of hope, and a little bit of courage, anything is possible.

So, let's raise a cup of tea, or a "Grande" coffee if you're feeling daring, and toast to the journey. Because in the end, it's not about the mistakes we make or the challenges we face, but about the memories we create and the lives we touch. And I am grateful for every step of this incredible journey, and for the opportunity to share it with all of you.

Dr. Dalal Akoury

Dr. Dalal Akoury, M.D. Founder of AWAREmed and Global Advanced Integrative Medicine Authority Almost 40 years' experience, working in almost 40 hospitals and clinics. Trains doctors worldwide in her highly effective methods, and helps them start and run their clinics.

Dr. Dalal can be reach at:

AwareMed.com & *PowerfulFemaleImmigrants.com*

EMPOWER WOMEN TO PURSUE THEIR DREAMS

Sherine Hanna, MD, Egypt

Lorem ipsum dolor sit amet, consectetur adipiscing elit. Sed ut sem quis purus pulvinar lobortis. Praesent ut congue urna. Aliquam posuere massa in tincidunt rutrum. Integer diam est, imperdiet nec mauris vitae, malesuada feugiat diam. Sed sollicitudin sapien ac orci blandit convallis. Donec id augue ut leo sagittis dictum. Sed in interdum libero.

Vestibulum sagittis, ipsum id commodo placerat, tellus massa vulputate orci, in auctor orci eros a nunc. Vestibulum ante ipsum primis in faucibus orci luctus et ultrices posuere cubilia curae; Quisque porttitor semper purus ac fringilla. Duis sem diam, maximus interdum nibh sit amet, suscipit convallis nulla. Vestibulum id massa felis. Vestibulum eget risus a nulla pharetra accumsan. Vestibulum ante ipsum primis in faucibus orci luctus et ultrices posuere cubilia curae; Duis vel finibus dolor. Vestibulum eget turpis ante. Aenean sit amet rutrum eros, sit amet malesuada felis. Integer feugiat mi leo.

Vivamus cursus felis mi, at pretium felis consequat nec. Duis sed porttitor ex. Mauris massa felis, facilisis sed vulputate sed, lacinia a dui. Curabitur arcu nunc, lobortis eget euismod eget, venenatis vitae urna. Aenean vestibulum dui a magna congue venenatis. Etiam arcu nisl, dapibus a convallis vitae, hendrerit sit amet nibh. Praesent turpis lorem, suscipit venenatis tincidunt sed, tempor pretium nunc. Aenean faucibus fringilla purus id interdum. Aenean porttitor consectetur nisl id aliquam. Donec eget ullamcorper nisi, quis posuere orci. Phasellus efficitur nunc ex, efficitur laoreet leo porta eget. Aenean pharetra ac augue et cursus.

Sed venenatis molestie maximus. Cras faucibus, odio at tristique porttitor, nibh nunc commodo ipsum, vel hendrerit erat dolor sit amet nunc. Donec mattis, purus sed interdum efficitur, nibh orci posuere lectus, quis luctus est felis at enim. Curabitur finibus tellus eu ultrices feugiat. Suspendisse commodo, metus vel lacinia efficitur, nisi diam venenatis urna, eget ultrices mi enim ac justo. Phasellus varius pretium elit nec finibus. Curabitur porta euismod nisi euismod consequat. Ut malesuada sollicitudin arcu sed viverra. Vivamus lacinia augue et efficitur finibus. Fusce et bibendum ligula. Phasellus posuere fringilla turpis, vitae dictum lectus blandit in. Integer eget egestas nunc. Duis dictum neque sem, vel condimentum ligula euismod nec.

Curabitur eu posuere nulla. Nunc ac sodales erat. Quisque consequat eget augue non eleifend. Morbi interdum justo eget tellus sollicitudin mollis. Mauris sit amet nulla non risus dictum eleifend sit amet eget arcu. Integer aliquet finibus ligula sed convallis. Proin a felis ante. Etiam eget ligula vel ipsum feugiat pharetra. Phasellus lacus eros, hendrerit nec sagittis in, mattis quis purus. Aenean sit amet velit pharetra, elementum mi in, feugiat mi. Donec diam nisl, lacinia quis ante sed, pulvinar tincidunt nibh.

Lorem ipsum dolor sit amet, consectetur adipiscing elit. Sed ut sem quis purus pulvinar lobortis. Praesent ut congue urna. Aliquam posuere massa in tincidunt rutrum. Integer diam est, imperdiet nec mauris vitae, malesuada feugiat diam. Sed sollicitudin sapien ac orci blandit convallis. Donec id augue ut leo sagittis dictum. Sed in interdum libero.

Vestibulum sagittis, ipsum id commodo placerat, tellus massa vulputate orci, in auctor orci eros a nunc. Vestibulum ante ipsum primis in faucibus orci luctus et ultrices posuere cubilia curae; Quisque porttitor semper purus ac fringilla. Duis sem diam, maximus interdum nibh sit amet, suscipit convallis nulla. Vestibulum id massa felis. Vestibulum eget risus a nulla pharetra accumsan. Vestibulum ante ipsum primis in faucibus orci luctus et ultrices posuere cubilia curae; Duis vel finibus dolor. Vestibulum eget turpis ante. Aenean sit amet rutrum eros, sit amet malesuada felis. Integer feugiat mi leo.

Vivamus cursus felis mi, at pretium felis consequat nec. Duis sed porttitor ex. Mauris massa felis, facilisis sed vulputate sed, lacinia a dui. Curabitur arcu nunc, lobortis eget euismod eget, venenatis vitae urna. Aenean vestibulum dui a magna congue venenatis. Etiam arcu nisl, dapibus a convallis vitae, hendrerit sit amet nibh. Praesent turpis lorem, suscipit venenatis tincidunt sed, tempor pretium nunc. Aenean faucibus fringilla purus id interdum. Aenean porttitor consectetur nisl id aliquam. Donec eget ullamcorper nisi, quis posuere orci. Phasellus efficitur nunc ex, efficitur laoreet leo porta eget. Aenean pharetra ac augue et cursus.

Sed venenatis molestie maximus. Cras faucibus, odio at tristique porttitor, nibh nunc commodo ipsum, vel hendrerit erat dolor sit amet nunc. Donec mattis, purus sed interdum efficitur, nibh orci posuere lectus, quis luctus est felis at enim. Curabitur finibus tellus eu ultrices feugiat. Suspendisse commodo, metus vel lacinia efficitur, nisi diam venenatis urna, eget ultrices mi enim ac justo. Phasellus varius pretium elit nec finibus. Curabitur porta euismod nisi euismod consequat. Ut malesuada sollicitudin arcu sed viverra. Vivamus lacinia augue et efficitur finibus. Fusce et bibendum ligula. Phasellus posuere fringilla turpis, vitae dictum lectus blandit in. Integer eget egestas nunc. Duis dictum neque sem, vel condimentum ligula euismod nec.

Curabitur eu posuere nulla. Nunc ac sodales erat. Quisque consequat eget augue non eleifend. Morbi interdum justo eget tellus sollicitudin mollis. Mauris sit amet nulla non risus dictum eleifend sit amet eget arcu. Integer aliquet finibus ligula sed convallis. Proin a felis ante. Etiam eget ligula vel ipsum feugiat pharetra. Phasellus lacus eros, hendrerit nec sagittis in, mattis quis purus. Aenean sit amet velit pharetra, elementum mi in, feugiat mi. Donec diam nisl, lacinia quis ante sed, pulvinar tincidunt nibh.

Lorem ipsum dolor sit amet, consectetur adipiscing elit. Sed ut sem quis purus pulvinar lobortis. Praesent ut congue urna. Aliquam posuere massa in tincidunt rutrum. Integer diam est, imperdiet nec mauris vitae, malesuada feugiat diam. Sed sollicitudin sapien ac orci blandit convallis. Donec id augue ut leo sagittis dictum. Sed in interdum libero.

Vestibulum sagittis, ipsum id commodo placerat, tellus massa vulputate orci, in auctor orci eros a nunc. Vestibulum ante ipsum primis in faucibus orci luctus et ultrices posuere cubilia curae; Quisque porttitor semper purus ac fringilla. Duis sem diam, maximus interdum nibh sit amet, suscipit convallis nulla. Vestibulum id massa felis. Vestibulum eget risus a nulla pharetra accumsan. Vestibulum ante ipsum primis in faucibus orci luctus et ultrices posuere cubilia curae; Duis vel finibus dolor. Vestibulum eget turpis ante. Aenean sit amet rutrum eros, sit amet malesuada felis. Integer feugiat mi leo.

Vivamus cursus felis mi, at pretium felis consequat nec. Duis sed porttitor ex. Mauris massa felis, facilisis sed vulputate sed, lacinia a dui. Curabitur arcu nunc, lobortis eget euismod eget, venenatis vitae urna. Aenean vestibulum dui a magna congue venenatis. Etiam arcu nisl, dapibus a convallis vitae, hendrerit sit amet nibh. Praesent turpis lorem, suscipit venenatis tincidunt sed, tempor pretium nunc. Aenean faucibus fringilla purus id interdum. Aenean porttitor consectetur nisl id aliquam. Donec eget ullamcorper nisi, quis posuere orci. Phasellus efficitur nunc ex, efficitur laoreet leo porta eget. Aenean pharetra ac augue et cursus.

Sed venenatis molestie maximus. Cras faucibus, odio at tristique porttitor, nibh nunc commodo ipsum, vel hendrerit erat dolor sit amet nunc. Donec mattis, purus sed interdum efficitur, nibh orci posuere lectus, quis luctus est felis at enim. Curabitur finibus tellus eu ultrices feugiat. Suspendisse commodo, metus vel lacinia efficitur, nisi diam venenatis urna, eget ultrices mi enim ac justo. Phasellus varius pretium elit nec finibus. Curabitur porta euismod nisi euismod consequat. Ut malesuada sollicitudin arcu sed viverra. Vivamus lacinia augue et efficitur finibus. Fusce et bibendum ligula. Phasellus posuere fringilla turpis, vitae dictum lectus blandit in. Integer eget egestas nunc. Duis dictum neque sem, vel condimentum ligula euismod nec.

About Dr. Sherine Hanna

Philosophy:

"Whatever you do work at it with all your heart"

"If you love what you do, you don't have to work a day in your life."

"Ma estahak an yea3eesh, man 3asha lenafseho fakat" Arabic for: He who lives only for himself does not deserve to live."

Vision: *To Collaborate with powerful, accomplished women to make a difference and to empower women to pursue their dreams

Since age 8, I was inspired to be a physician as I was fascinated with how the human body works and wanted to figure out its complexity.

This desire intensified when I almost lost my brother to an electrocution accident. Endless prayers and really admiring the physicians and nurses and how they saved his life made me further confident of my medical path.

My father always told me that I was able to do anything that I set my mind to. He believed in me, which made me believe in myself.

My parents wanted to give us a better life as well as religious and social freedom

As a new immigrant at the beginning of high school, I struggled with fitting in, learning a new culture while keeping my career dream alive.

I looked up to other doctors in the community. They tried to discourage me as I was a new immigrant and I needed to excel to gain admission to medical school.

They said as an immigrant woman that would someday start a family, this was not very realistic dream.

They told me that there were lots of sacrifices and it would only be worthwhile if I loved it, and I did love it.

I am a solution oriented person, with the ability to see past short term and individual needs in favor of broader long-term positive results and impact for humanity.

I excelled and became a physician. I chose the field of anesthesia as an epidural that I personally had while in labor, completely eliminated my pain, and I knew that was amazing gift to offer.

My brother got Leukemia when he was 38, and I was his perfect match

I was thankful that I had the medical knowledge to help him and be by his side.

He did pass away 5 years later. A part of my heart was forever aching, but that just drove me to feel what my patients feel, and to have empathy.

I used my anesthesia career to comfort patients as they went through major operations

I specialized in doing nerve blocks to help block their pain.

I published papers in my field.

I was involved in mentoring medical students and residents.

I am currently the Illinois president for the National Arab American Medical Association. It is an amazing opportunity to mentor younger physicians, and to fund raise for noble causes as well as help international students.

As a medical mentor, I think the most important thing that I hope to impart my passion and enthusiasm for medicine and for empowering my patients.

I am now the chief of anesthesia for few hospitals and am very involved across our healthcare system to redesign systems in order to improve safety and provide access to healthcare for patients.

Whatever I do, there is always a smile as I feel very fortunate to be in this position to be able to make a difference. I want to show my patients compassion and offer them a smile and pain relief during their worst times.

I went back to Egypt, my home country, last summer.

Something was different. I felt that I was called to be there.

I did buy a couple of properties there and plan to spend part of my retirement there.

I am teaming up with Dr Akoury to help alleviate pain for cancer patients and to also help empower people to take control of their health and well-being.

Dr. Sherine can be reach at:

sherinehanna@hotmail.com & *PowerfulFemaleImmigrants.com*

LET'S GOOOOOOO!

Julia Valentine, Latvia

As a child growing up in Latvia, I loved it when my mom read books to me every night before I went to sleep. In what I'm fairly certain is my first conscious memory of myself at three years old, I still remember the evening when she read me the story that entranced me. I can't remember the exact book she read, but before finishing the very last page, she closed the book and said, "If you want to learn more, you need to learn how to read." She did teach me the letters before, of course.

To say that it piqued my curiosity is to say absolutely nothing. I couldn't sleep. Somehow, I managed to read the last page. It felt like a monumental effort, but when I did it, I felt elated. What I learned at three years old is that I could figure out anything, that the process of doing so was the coolest thing, and that no cheap substitute would suffice.

When I started first grade, I showed up at school with the *Forsyte Saga,* a book whose author won the Nobel Prize in literature (I could not put it down, but my first-grade teacher rolled her eyes and asked me to bring *The Three Musketeers* instead), and I passed the time reading my books and helping the teacher grade homework. My parents are classically trained musicians, and seeing how bored I was at school, they enrolled me into an additional full-time music school, where I studied music theory, played the piano and accompanied a violin—with my days starting at 7 a.m. and ending at 11 p.m.

I was born in Latvia before it became independent, and the quality of my inner life was completely at odds with the dull, robotic reality of socialism. Another memory—when I was nine years old—reading about the pyramids of Egypt in *The Seven Wonders of the World* and thinking to myself, "How is it possible that I'm not allowed to leave my country and see the pyramids with my own eyes?" I was reading a chapter on the Great Wall of China and, I swear, a thought came into my mind as clear as if someone next to me said, "You will see it." In 2003, I was standing on the Great Wall of China—I did it! As Audrey Hepburn said, "Nothing is impossible, the word, itself, says I'm possible."

Latvia became independent when I was fourteen years old, and my family could leave, but they were afraid to venture into the unknown. The twentieth century was not kind to our kin. My great-grandmother was five years old when her parents starved, and she became a servant to a family that made her work for food. She married an officer who was sent to Gulag by Stalin. My grandmother, her daughter, almost starved growing up during World War II, and yet became a doctor and later managed thousands of doctors in dozens of locations—my role model in everything. Some of our family-owned land and windmills (early ESG) and paid for it with their lives when 39 of them, including women and children, were drowned by people who took their property and their lives. My paternal grandmother, born in Latvia, spent three years in a death camp called Ravensbruck during World War II and survived. She was trusted with dividing up the food between everyone in her barrack—my other role model of impeccable honesty even in the face of death. And the list goes on and on. What I saw when socialism ended is that none of these crimes were discussed or acknowledged, and the same type of people stayed in power. I pushed my family to leave.

We applied to a family reunification program in the United States and waited for an interview for four long years. During that time, Latvia was in the process of legally gaining its independence. If that process reversed, our names would be on the list of people wanting to get out—a potential death sentence. The day Russian tanks rolled into my city, Riga, sent chills to our bones. My friends and I went into the town square and stood a few short steps away from the barrel of a tank pointed at us. I knew the physical fear that generations of my family before me had experienced, and my determination to get us out was unshakable. I was born with high energy and resilience, and the risk was worth being taken. As we kept waiting, Latvia became independent, but we faced a new hurdle: we became stateless because we couldn't apply for the Latvian citizenship while waiting to go to the U.S.

During this time, I graduated from a specialized math and physics high school with straight A's (including my first programming class) and spent two years studying linguistics in a dual English and German program at the foreign language's faculty of the University of Latvia. I studied Latin and Semiotics, read *Beowulf* in Old English and Friedrich Nietzsche in the original. While it seemed like we waited forever, these four years further opened me to culture and languages.

I knew that my English needed to be fluent by the time we made it to New York, and I studied incessantly.

We finally made it to the United States, and I got to know the price the first-generation immigrants pay. We spent seven years being stateless. My family had to leave behind all our property—Latvia didn't allow us to sell it, and it didn't allow us to take cash or valuables out of the country (yes, it was before crypto). We lost our social capital— the friendships, the community, the connections. Working through the emotional side of things was the most difficult part because we had family and friends who stayed in Latvia, and since it was before the internet age, we had little means of connecting with them. This complete misery of losing status, money, and friends moved me to look inside and figure out what really makes me—and how to make my life substantial without the stuff. It took me a while, but I'm almost always in a good mood because my only prerequisite is being alive. I really do keep the bar low. Anything else is just icing on a cake.

When I came to New York City, my most pressing task was continuing my education. I don't know how I did it because it was insane to accomplish it in my first three months in the country, but I managed to enroll in New York University as a transfer student from the University of Latvia, although my two years with a GPA of 4.0 translated into four credits (one course) at NYU. Still, my preparation paid off. When I took my English as a Second Language test at NYU, it turned out I didn't need to take any ESL—I joined the regular program. I also took the foreign language requirement test in German and fully passed, which freed up an entire extra semester, so I did a double major—economics and finance. I was invited to join an advanced economics program that was quantitative—we used mathematics, statistics, econometrics, and programming in our studies and thesis—and I earned the NYU Jacob Marschak Memorial Award for Excellence in Quantitative Analysis/Econometrics for my thesis on the relationship between economic freedom and prosperity. I loved every class I took at NYU. My curiosity in financial markets, economics, and other subjects that I took made it an exciting time for me. I had to work 35 hours a week as a bookkeeper and take out loans to afford NYU. I slept four hours a night. But when I graduated NYU Stern School of Business *magna cum laude*, I was invited to join Beta Gamma Sigma, the Honor Society for Schools of Business and Omicron Delta Epsilon, International Honor Society in Economics. Despite being exhausted, I felt I had a major victory. I turned my attention to finding something I could absolutely love doing.

During my last semester of NYU, I interviewed with Lacy Hunt, then Chief Economist U.S.A. at HSBC, who hired me as a research assistant. I spent the year at HSBC trying to decide whether I wanted to pursue a PhD in Economics, while doing research and even some basic forecasting. Fortunately for me, Wall Street was going through the Y2K exercise (the year 2000 error), and I got hired by Prudential Securities to work on fixed income trading systems and portfolio modeling. I loved fintech. If you combine curiosity, complexity, creativity, and efficiency, that is just what fintech means to me. I was very lucky to find my path so quickly. I got to work on some high-profile projects with a lot of smart people, and we had fun, too.

After a few years with Prudential, I carefully mapped my next step: find a firm where I can learn equities and that would pay for my MBA. I took my GMAT, a graduate school admissions test, without studying and three years before I needed it. I figured that it was a great idea to take it without any time pressure, since, at the time, it was valid for five years. An opportunity with J.P. Morgan came up. I didn't get it. I figured I was 25 and looked inexperienced and unimpressive. A year later, a similar position with J.P. Morgan came up. I dyed my blonde hair black and wore the most conservative suit I could find. I got the job, elated that my business address was 60 Wall Street. My first project was so successful that J.P. Morgan Investment Bank Technology CTO signed off on my executive MBA—J.P. Morgan covered the cost of my MBA and gave me every Friday off to attend classes. I got to continue with my career, had no debt, and studied at Columbia University with accomplished executives, many of whom I am privileged to have as my friends and support network. And our class trip was to Hong Kong and China, including the Great Wall.

Everything that I just described happened in my first ten years in New York. I don't think there is any other place on this planet where an immigrant woman could go from a zero start to being a VP at J.P. Morgan with an executive MBA from Columbia University in ten years. I am entrepreneurial by nature, but I had a strong feeling that getting some experience from well-established firms would do me good. I learned everything I could, and I looked for the best firms to learn from. My next opportunity came when I was recruited into a hedge fund called D. E. Shaw; it was considered number one in the world at the time I joined it. D. E. Shaw demanded exceptional quality of work in everything, including communication. Becoming meticulous in the quality of my verbal and written communication was very, very difficult for me. English as a second language did not cut it. I had nightmares that I was on TV, was asked a question, and didn't understand what I was being asked.

Here is where I got lucky: I met my yoga teacher, Tahji Beth LaComb (check out her awesome site at YogaBeesAreBeautiful.com), a really great coach, Marina Ilyn, our amazing teacher, Mira, and our yoga group. They taught me how to balance achievement, enjoyment, and service, and how to work with my body, mind, emotions, and spirit.

This helped a lot with raising a child in New York City—such an amazing place for kids. We have an amazing group of family, friends, parents, teachers, and a support network and a shield around our kids. Parents, Beatrice, Masha, Lenny, Julia, Nika, Sam, Olga, Alex, Jason, Dhira, Tira, Giuliana, Carmelinda, Miguel, Beth, Robbie, Tracy, Mike, Grace, Samrah, Jenny, Sai Suhas, Ayesha, Jerry, Danielle, Lynn, Tara, Anita, Adam, Scott, Celia, Libby, Michael, Vita, Phoebe, Brittini, Mark, Brinkley, Marty, Jennifer, Jessica, Joelle, Maya, Fatima, Meghan, Sami, Paula, Felix, Rita, Anthony, Maria, Tai, Lea, Jackie, Adam, Success Academy teachers and staff, and many others—you know who you are—thank you!

It seems simple to me now—with each step, I needed to master new skillsets. But it wasn't as obvious to me back then. Now, I have a PhD in starting at zero and building up to significant achievement. I don't know if it equates to losing your ego, but I think, on some level, it is a key to entrepreneurship. You can have a C-level position, start your own company, and suddenly you need to learn how to sell—something that was excruciatingly difficult for me for the first two years, and now I love it. If there is one thing that I am going to teach my daughter, it is not to be afraid to start from zero, get comfortable with being uncomfortable while building your skills, be supportive of yourself while doing it, and giving yourself the runway to learn and then succeed, and then keep going. Want to get inspired? Look at these facts:

- 55 percent of U.S. unicorns (startups with a value over $1 billion) were founded by immigrants.

- 45 percent of Fortune 500 companies were founded by immigrants.

- Immigrants account for about 25 percent of U.S. entrepreneurship and innovation.

- Immigrant graduates with STEM degrees are twice as likely to file for a patent.

I am very supportive of people who are doers, and I am not in the habit of criticizing them—I know how it feels and what it takes to achieve. My appreciation of people who set high goals for themselves and keep going after them is immense. And as far as dealing with my nightmare of looking silly on TV, I wrote a book and went on actual radio and TV interviews (I got to see the actual NPR studio, that was cool)… and after the first twenty or so interviews, my fear was gone forever.

I got to work for other great firms, including a top-ten family office and a large pension fund with $110 billion in assets under management, where I was a chief technology officer and a chief operating officer. I am currently the CTO and COO at AlphaMille, a global technology consulting firm serving investment funds, family offices, and startups. Our company builds technology spanning from fintech to metaverse, blockchain, and AI. I am grateful to work with highly accomplished, intelligent, and kind business partners who have an unconditional positive regard for everyone around them.

I co-founded a think tank called the Digital Evolution Institute, which brings together the brightest stars in their fields to examine how technology is transforming various parts of our lives—from the future of food to the future of AI, aviation, robotics, mental health, management, space… and even the future of death. I am still doing yoga and meditation, so I have my own thoughts on that topic. Whatever happens in the beyond, I'm giving myself three months to figure it out once I get there. And if time doesn't exist there, or there is some other hang-up, so be it—I think I'll just be looking for my tribe. At this point, life is about people, not territory.

Julia Valentine

Julia Valentine is the managing partner at AlphaMille.com and the co-founder of the Digital Evolution Institute. She is a board member of the Apple Bank and an advisor to *ConnectOurKids.com, YogaBeesAreBeautiful. com, Winpra.com* and *NextGenLeaderGroup. com.*

Julia can be reach at:

DigitalEvolution.institute & *PowerfulFemaleImmigrants.com*

A CHILD OF THE REVOLUTION

Heidi Rios, Nicaragua

Hola, hola! is the Heidi home? My neighbor friends would come and yell hello at my door to ask my dad if I could play on the street. No need to set up a play date, call you in advance or ask for permission. Just show up to live and play! During the revolution in Nicaragua, we did not have a lot of things. We did not have a lot of food or clothes or toys. What we had a lot of, was comradery, solidarity, endurance and for me, the most precious of all, we knew how to have fun. No matter what!

We would create anything that did not exist. For baseball, you would get a stick for the bat and a deodorant plastic container filled with dirt for the ball. And voila! Best baseball matches every day. No toys? No problem. You can catch mosquitoes. It was my favorite! My older brother would be in my team! The coolest kid on the block who happen to be my brother would be in my team. We would be the strongest team that could kill the most mosquitos. You would know you win by counting the blood spots on the wall. You can find any excuse or any way to have fun. I do not remember once feeling bored or uninspired. There was always a piece of junk or bugs to tinker with and have the most fun. Nicaraguans really live up to the American saying "when life gives you lemons, make lemonade".

My Passion For Learning and Teaching

As a little girl, I had this unshakable passion for languages. English was my obsession. I taught myself this practical and perfect language for business. I remember singing songs I had no idea what the words were or what they meant! I was Completely obsessed with 80's music that nobody would understand. I remember the first time I was able to sing a song from beginning to end just by listening and repeating over and over again. Dictionary in hand! "Every rose has its thorn "by Poison. I felt like graduating from college! I taught myself a whole song in a whole new language!

As you might guess, I went to college to learn English! I graduated from the University of Central America in Nicaragua with a bachelor's degree in English translation. I never worked professionally as a translator. Instead, I decided to take a master's degree in education. Another passion of mine. Nothing makes me feel more truly alive than learning and teaching. I happen to believe that the best way to learn is to teach everything you know.

I am addicted to learning. My passion for it began with languages. I taught myself English, I studied French, I really became addicted to German and after my crazy adventure, a mom, a toddler and a baby in China, we found ourselves feeling fond of Chinese. I read somewhere that when you learn a new language, it is like getting another soul. I really think so! Learning languages opened big doors for my endeavors as professional educator, a world traveler and now a businesswoman in real estate. Financial freedom and the means to change the world; my next mountain to climb!

Opening My Soul Against Stigmas

I grew up hating Americans. They were mean and evil. They were killing Nicaraguans. They were sending weapons under the table to abolish communism. They were terrorists.

I saw so many moms cry and faint in the streets in front of me for having lost their children who were fighting in the war. I was not sure how I could help them. I became famous in my country by reciting poetry for the martyrs and our people fighting for peace and freedom. In my poetry I would say " no more red Christmas, bring white Christmas", " Prepare your sling shot my little David that Goliath is waiting for you", " In my mind I weave and unweave a new shirt to protect you from bullets, it can't be pierced by thorny bushed and you can't be seen by la contra" the counter revolution right wing rebels who were funded by U.S. The war between the contras and the Sandinistas ended with a cease-fire in 1990.

I really believed that Americans were responsible for this tragedy. Little I knew, I would fall in love with the beautiful people of the land of the free and the home of the brave. I understood that our suffering had nothing to do with the people. It was their government who was supporting the contras, not the citizens.

When I became, I am American citizen, I felt invincible, and I knew that there was not thing I could not do! I think that America is the greatest country in the world. The opportunities I have found here could not possibly be given to me in my own country or another place on earth. I can travel the world. I can buy houses on my own. I can have the career I love. I can be a successful entrepreneur. I will forever be thankful for this country that allows me to be the woman I want to be. I love to come back from other places in the world to the airports in American land, with the feeling that I am home! I love your carefree attitude, confidence and welcoming to other cultures. Because it is just a reduced group that do not welcome others. America is also known as the melting pot for a reason.

Learning To Fly Solo Without A Safety Net-
The Strongest Wings Ever!

Taking full responsibility for my actions and without blaming absolutely anybody; I found myself lost and with nobody to run to when my marriage fell apart. I am deeply grateful for the many, many years of loneliness and darkness that forced me to find the strength and the courage to pick myself up.

It was hard to reach out and seek for support. I was ashamed to be a divorcee and I was reluctant to make new friends. It took me almost a decade to pick up the pieces of me and build my own wings. Give hugs to your younger self. Tell her that your mistakes do not define you, that the judgement of others do not matter more than your opinion of yourself. At the end of the day, you will shine through because it is you the only one responsible for your own path. Nobody else will build your wings for you and the sooner that you can do that, the sooner your will continue your path to greatness, with the strongest wings ever.

We all have within the absolute power of the human spirit. There are times in life that we cannot change a situation, but we can change our attitudes. Like the women in this book, they all have learned "how to suffer" if needed be. I go as far to argue that the greatest people are not necessarily the great athletes not the great scientists or public figures held in highest regard, but the people that hold their heads high having overcome incredible hardships.

Don't you feel like a victim. Ever! Instead, find gratitude for all the battles you overcome. And hold up your head high for the incredible tenacity that makes the superhuman that you choose to be! What an incredible opportunity to reinvent yourself!

There is Not a Thing a Mom Cannot Do

I became a mother of two amazing children that show me how to love fiercely. Always forgiving and enthusiastic about this beautiful world. For me, motherhood is the greatest call, the ultimate thing. You are this invincible creature that can sing the alphabet in all the languages, sleep on a bed of bed of nails and cross intercontinental oceans swimming. I loved giving birth. I felt like a wild beast. I really think that women who become moms lose their marbles a little bit. It is not possible to handle this love in your body bigger than the world!

My family lives abroad. I chose to leave Nicaragua. I am far from them and I totally accept motherhood without family support. I chose my path and I have no regrets. This is not about blaming or complaining. I take full responsibility of my choices. I gave birth twice without my family. I raise my children without the support of the village they say it takes. I woke up every morning with a small toddler and a new born with zero sleep only to go to work whether it was snowing or raining fire. Long hours back and forth in heavy traffic for pickups and drop-offs at daycare and school for years and years, no breaks, no rest, doing it all over again day after day. Laundry, cleaning, feeding, playing, entertaining, stimulating crafty games; Mary Poppins syndrome and all. A mom never stops. I get a big kiss and a bear hug every day when I pick them up from school. Eyes wide open and the most enthusiastic jump to hug me. It does not get old. Who would not walk the dessert to be hugged like that?

You get to do more things and it is more amazing as the difficulties get bigger so does your strength. God give kids supernatural moms when they do not have the village that it takes to raise children.

We have been traveling all over the world always together in remote place. The 3 musketeers, making unforgettable moments from seeing magma peeking into active volcanoes to climbing the great wall of China, my absolute favorite travel buddies to see the world. I want to tell all mamas, that traveling with small babies to the other side of the world is not only possible but it is also easy! It is easier than what we already do at home. You get pampered. You do not have to cook or do laundry and you do not have to drive! You would be amazed to experience faraway places can also feel like home. I say you give it a try!

My story is not unique. I am speaking for every queen mom out there that will never drop the ball even if it is raining fire. I want to tell all warrior moms out there that when you feel the guilt creeping up on you, find a moment to cradle your pain like a precious baby and recognize that you are:

A Beautiful woman
A good mom
Not mediocre

A warrior of life and love
A strong queen mom
More than enough

My Soul Keeps Getting Younger

I am an immigrant like millions of people that came to this country for a better future. An educator at heart, passionate and forever hungry for learning, for bigger and greater things.

I started my teaching career at rough school. Going back to work everyday was a miracle but I had the best school preparation of a lifetime.

I moved to other school systems. Things got so, so easy. I had the best school preparation of a lifetime. Dealing with difficult kids prepares you to win battles that only titans can conquer. I have been working at the different school now for more than 10 years. I really do not have the words to describe the kind of learners I work with. Little warriors, dreamers, easily encouraged, easy to smile, dedicated language learners, hard-working, kick butt kind of people. Supportive, empathetic, extremely smart, with incredible work ethic, real, tenacious. Extremely poised to hit it out of the park. Sure, I have students that struggle to invest in their own success. That is what adults are supposed to be there for. To guide them, inspire them, encourage them. But most importantly to help them with those battles humans are confronted with in the day to day. Fear, limiting beliefs, fixed mindset, self-defeat. Have we all not been there? Even as adults! Kids are best kind of people. I think I work with the best kids of America. Working daily with warrior kids just keeps you forever young. Learning, teaching, supporting, laughter, karaoke, music, silly videos, Zumba, Salsa, , yodeling, goofing off, presentational speaking tasks, final exam preparation, speeches from climate change to myths and legends in the world, comradery, growth, togetherness, common struggles, common dreams, meeting with success, doing whatever it takes to help one another succeed. It is an everyday classroom overflowing with miracles!

My Very Next Mountain

I am deeply thankful for this amazing journey called life. I never lose my hunger. I never want to stop climbing mountains. My dreams keep getting bigger and bigger! My dream is to reach out to children at greater risks. People that are consider lesser and that the whole world has given up on them. I am absolutely convinced that anybody who is given the opportunity to better their lives with love and unshakable determination can become agents of change themselves. There is research of cases that people survive terminal diseases because they make up their minds that they are going to live! Let's look at winners who refuse to be limited by their genetic handicap. People from the most difficult environments who become extraordinary winners and impressively splendid achievers. They are living proof that you create your reality. You create your luck, your state of mind, your health, your wealth! I love to learn about testimonials by people who against all odds win their battles. They are my inspiration to follow my fantasies. I want to change the world. I want to surround myself with positive thinkers and dreamers like me who want to make a difference in this world.

I have been learning everything I can about real estate and multifamily syndication. I went from a flip project with a group of fearless women to 200 doors in multifamily in 1 year! As I am writing these electronic words, I am already congratulating myself for the next 120 doors my out-of-this-world syndication team and I will close next month. What a roller coaster you go through when you choose to do hard things so you can create your reality. I would not have it any other way. Success is not a surprise. You know you are going to get there because you will not give up. I love what my mentor says all the time " If you are committed to the activity, success is inevitable". It is very important to have a clear vision of your goals and a team you absolutely depend on. Education and execution equals power. But what you absolutely need to have to grab life by the throat is the mindset to do the impossible.

1. **Education**
2. **Mentorship**
3. **Network like crazy**
4. **Find your dream team**
5. **Take massive action (or one foot in front of the other)**
6. **Be a difference maker**

My goal is to become a wealth builder and positively impact people's lives. Filthy rich, powerful me. This is where I am going to go! Real estate is my vehicle to get there. I am currently hell bent-decided to educate myself and others on how to demystify the impossibility of becoming wealthy and financially free through real estate investing. The safest way on the planet to grow your wealth. Like Miguel de Cervantes called it " There are no limits but the sky"

The right mindset can take you far in life. There is not a thing you cannot do! My goal is to give away a million dollars many times around. I want to go back to Nicaragua and pick up all the kids from the streets in Managua. One million kids, One million meals, One million people in need. I truly believe that the meaning of life is beyond ourselves. We are meant to be here to make the world a better place. Life is meaningful when we know that we are doing things that matter. We experience incredible satisfaction when we live with purpose beyond satisfying our selfish needs. The more we do things to create impact and serve others, the bigger the probability of experiencing true happiness.

I want to end this part of this book about my life with a beautiful quote from Pope Francis "Life is not worth living if you do not live to serve"

Heidi Rios

- My degree is from University of Central America in Nicaragua
- I did my MBA in Education at Framingham, MA
- Teaching Foreign Languages to high school students. My biggest homerun

has been working with human minds. Connecting with super interesting people for the last 20 years of my life. I am never going to stop teaching.

My most recent endeavor now is to become a stellar capital raiser and investor relations for my team and investors whose foundation is to grow together.

- My ideal team and I have in common: Passion, experience and integrity.

I am Heidi Rios from Nicaragua. I am an educator, a real estate investor, capital raiser, a creator and an implementor. I have become a warrior determined to achieve success in financial freedom. I have been living in Baltimore, MD for 10 years. I am a mom of two small kids with whom I have been traveling the world since they were in my belly. We just came back from the jungle in Central America a few weeks ago! We saw magma a few feet away from us! We can't get enough of exploring the world. There is not a thing a mom cannot do!

Heidi can be reach at:

instagram.com/InvestAtTheNextLevel.com
PowerfulFemaleImmigrants.com

BREAKING FREE:
A MINORITY WOMAN'S COURAGEOUS JOURNEY TO ACHIEVING HER DREAMS IN AMERICA

Helen Mastanduno, Malaysia

Petaling Jaya, Malaysia My Hometown

I was born in Ipoh, Perak, and raised in a big city called Petaling Jaya, Selangor, Malaysia that the townspeople call PJ. I grew up the youngest of three siblings in a suburban areaacross the street from a huge rolling field of plains where people would go and play soccer with their peers. My parents were hard workers who did everything to take care of us and see that wereceived the education that they weren't able to receive. My mother was a hardworking housewife who loved to cook for the college students who rented out our extra room. My father drove taxis and owned a hotel that did well enough to provide a comfortable life for us all.

I was an adventurous kid who loved to explore and try new things. As a young girl, I would take my little bike that matched my petite stature and roll all over my neighborhood to visit my friends, the store to buy snacks, and anywhere my little bike would take me. When I gotolder, I would often sneak out to hang out with much older men to ride on their Harley Davidsons, telling my mother that I was going to work at my part-time job or asking my friend, whom I called my cousin, who lived with us at the time, to open the back door and cover me as I got picked up by these older men, one of whom went by the name of Moe. These nightly adventures were the highlight of my teenage years, until I got caught. One morning, my brother stood in front of the door waiting for me at 5 a.m. As I pulled up, my eyes widened, and my heart raced as I realized the show was over. I was restricted from going out for a long time by my parents, who believed it was my friend negatively influencing me, although it was both of us walking on the wild side. I used many excuses to sneak out, such as pretending to go towork as an excuse to hang out with the "Harley gang." These were fond times that I would soonleave behind to go on an even bigger adventure. An adventure that would last a lifetime on American soil.

Coming to America

As I boarded the plane, leaving everything I have known for 19 years behind, reality shook me as I took one last look at my native home, hugged my family, then boarded the plane. A river of tears flowed from my eyes the entire flight as I contended with the mixed emotions ofleaving behind everything I knew and being excited about the amazing adventure ahead of me. Icouldn't imagine what life would be like without my mother's cooking, my father's yelling, my siblings ratting me out, my partner in crime, whom I call my best friend, and the wild nights of PJ nightlife with the Harley gang. The next chapter of my life would soon unfold in a series ofevents that would shape my future.

My First Steps on American Soil

When I landed and the dust settled, I was so happy, thinking to myself, "Oh my God, I am finally free!" Although I would miss everyone back home, I no longer had to worry about my parents nagging me about going out. I could do as I pleased and have all the freedom that I wanted! AsI looked around, excited and overwhelmed at the same time, my attention was caught by the skycap, who offered to help me with my luggage, which I obliged. Once I got to my next destination, he stood there staring at me and then began to curse me out like a sailor! "Blank blank, you could've given me a blankety blank tip after I helped you!" was all I could hear.

Puzzled, I wondered why he was so angry, then I heard the end part of his sentence about a tip.Welcome to America, I guess! I learned a valuable lesson about tipping that day!

America was a world totally different from PJ. Everything compared to PJ was bigger, such as the food, the clothes, the people, and the attitudes! Everything made me look like an ant among grasshoppers. I had a lot of adjustments to make. I found the nearest mall to explore because I wanted to see the fashion America had to offer. One of the first stores that caught my eye was a lingerie store. I walked in, and my jaw instantly dropped at what my eyes beheld. I picked up a bra, and my eyes popped out, as I had never seen one so big! I took the bra and put itover my head, where it fit perfectly. It was then that I realized I was in over my head, (pun intended).

College Life Extravaganza

I arrived here in August 1993 to go to Johnson & Wales University, located in Providence, Rhode Island. As a young child growing up, I always wanted to work in a hotel, as I admired my father's accomplishments and wanted to follow in his footsteps. This influenced me to choose the major of hotel, restaurant, and institutional management. I met this guy at the international house, and after a brief conversation, we decided to share an apartment. He was a man about 10 years older than me and from Sweden. Since I was no stranger to older men, and barely afraid of anything, this didn't seem like much of a risk at the time. I recall one year during college break, I decided to go to Los Angeles to visit my friend. I rented a car to visit another friend of ours in San Francisco. During our time there, we had an absolute ball until it was time to drive back. Upon our departure from California, we got into a terrible accident, totaling the rental! I injured my hip, and my friend had minor cuts and bruises, but I dared not go to the emergency room. I was terrified because I did not have insurance at the time, and I was more afraid of being yelled at by my dad than taking care of my injury. At the time, the only thing that mattered was staying incognito. We got another rental in this small town on the way back to L.A. but had to end up driving back to the small town because my friend's name wasn't on the rental. So, there I was, injured, got back, and had to leave to go back to school in Providence. The next morning, I started driving to the airport and ended up in San Diego because I was given the wrong directions and wound up missing my flight. This was a total nightmare that I guess balanced out the fun we had. My time in school was adventurous. I didn't stay on campus in dorms, which I somewhat regret, however, I ended up making friends from all over the world and enjoyed my college days.

I'm Done with College, Now What?

After college graduation, my friend, who had moved to New York from Malaysia, and I decided to move to an apartment in Brooklyn, New York. We rented a U-Haul, packed up, and off we went, despite a blizzard warning. So, there I was, this tiny 4'11" Asian gal, driving a big U- Haul truck, barely tall enough to see over the steering wheel, hauling across town to a new state, in the middle of a historic 1995 blizzard. Our apartment had no fridge, no furniture, no stove, nothing. We ended up having to leave everything outside in the U-Haul and sleep on the cold floor with nothing except what we wore on the way in. After the snow subsided, we were able to comfortably move our things into our apartment and set out to find our first jobs after graduation.

I landed my first job after college at the airport as the concession manager at the TWA terminal at John F. Kennedy International Airport in New York. I was the only Asian person working in that sector of the airport, and my coworkers would call me "One Dolla, One Dolla!" as they teased and laughed, and I lightheartedly laughed with them. I never took offense, as I saw it as a funny joke. I enjoyed my time there and moved on to work at a well-known diner as a restaurant manager in NYC called EJ's Luncheonette. During my time there, I had the pleasure of meeting many well-known celebrities such as, Joe Torre, the Yankees manager, Wayne Gretzky, a famous ice hockey player, and Ben Stiller, an actor known for his comedic roles. I met amazing people and enjoyed some amazing food. As a foodie, I appreciated the delicious freebies I enjoyed on the daily basis. It was an amazing experience that I'll never forget.

I met my then husband at the tender age of 23 and decided to get married to be able to stay in the United States. It was a quick decision that I made at a very young age that seemed convenient for both me and him. We had our child together and would often get into fights due to his mother wanting our child to always be with her. She wanted another child of her own and chose to repeatedly keep our child overnight. He would often leave us alone to go be with her, which led me to have frequent panic attacks at the hands of the constant conflict and fighting. I begged him to go seek counseling, and he refused. I grew weary of the constant war that went on within the walls of my home. I threw in the towel and called it quits on the marriage. He finally wanted to seek counseling, but it was too late, I had had enough. I decided to never do that again. After seven years of marriage, we decided to mutually part ways and filed for divorce.

As a now single mother going through a divorce, I was struggling to pay my mortgage and had to work three to four jobs to pay my bills. I had a full-time job working in insurance during the day and worked at multiple gyms after work, teaching exercise classes and providing personal training seven days a week. There were times that my bank account would have two dollars in it after paying all the bills. I hit my lowest point when all of this began to affect my son. I married young and wasn't able to enjoy single life after college. Immediately after my divorce, I would party every weekend. I would have my ex-husband watch my son, even if it was my turn to have him. One day, I was lying in bed next to my 10-year-old son. He turned to me and looked me in the eyes with so much desperation and said, "Mom, I wish you would spend more time with me." I was crushed. How could I spend so much time at work and partying that I neglected to give my time to the one person in the world who mattered the most to me? I felt like a terrible mother. From that day on, I gave up the partying and gave my time back to my son, where it belonged, and I made sure when I had him that I spent as much time with him as possible. Today, he is 22 years old, and our relationship is so amazing. I am so grateful for what happened because, without those struggles, our relationship would not be where it is today.

I had many relationships that puzzled me, as I didn't grasp the whirlwind of differences in what relationships meant in these new lands compared to what I was used to back home. I found myself in relationship after relationship that went nowhere. In one particular relationship, I dated this Harley biker on and off for five years. He was mentally, emotionally, and verbally abusive. I was trauma-bonded with this man, who captivated me with his bad boy style. I was so in love with him and thought he would be the one. He had never been married and probably had no intentions of ever getting married. I was so blinded by the thrill and excitement of being with him that I wasted precious years of my time. I was heartbroken, financially broke, and time broke. Life didn't seem to go anywhere. I almost filed for bankruptcy three times, but glory be, two angels came to my rescue: my sister and my now husband.

My Forever Family

Me and my now husband started off rocky. My in-laws were apprehensive about our relationship, and we met great resistance due to the constant conflict. I met my husband three weeks after the passing of his late wife, and I was believed by his family to be his mistress. The first year was quite the challenge, as I went from having one child and being single for 12 years to having three children and being married. Dealing with the conflict of his family vacillating between the grief they endured and supporting their son caused me to be caught in the middle of a war I did not create. The adjustment of mothering multiple small children was no easy task while having this conflict hovering above my head daily. My husband and I constantly fought because of the berating I endured from his family. I stepped into the role of becoming the motherof two young grieving children, caught in the crossfire of pain I could not fathom, but wanted to love them to a place of healing. I had to find a way to be the soothing balm for a grieving spouse,heartbroken children, and a reassurance for in-laws who had their own way of dealing with the tragedy. I chose to forgive for my own peace, and now his family and I are harmonious, and we love each other to pieces. The first few years of my marriage were not easy, but love won in the end and continues to be the driving force of our family unit.

My Experience Full Circle

Although I miss my hometown tremendously, including my friends, my family, and the food, it was worth the risk, as I have gained such a beautiful family and had an amazing journey. America came with no instruction manual. I had to adapt as time went on. I took risks, made mistakes, I had fun, shed tears, and grew like a flower breaking through the concrete. When I was 19, I never thought in a million years that I would become who I am today. Today, I have to say that I have much more than I ever could have dreamed of. I am going to push myself even harder to get to the next level in my career.

A pivotal point in my career was when I had a spiritual awakening and received my calling to give back and help others. When I was going through financial hardships, I struggled in silence and dared to tell no one. Today, financially, I am in a better situation, and I have decided to help women. I have set up a nonprofit called Hope and Love, Inc. to help homeless veteran women find housing and equip them with the necessary skills to live fulfilling lives. The heroes that fought for our country paved the way for me to be able to come to America and live in peace, and it is time for us to fight for them. Some of my other accomplishments include becoming a P.C. Real Estate New Jersey State President and the owner of a branch office, having a cooking show called *Homemade with Hel* that airs globally on Boss Ladies TV Network, and currently working on my third business that I have started under the mentorship of a billionaire investor! Things are going very well for me at this time of my life and are only getting better!

If you are one who is afraid of taking risks, look at my life as an example of what bravery can bring about. If you enjoyed this story, be sure to follow me on my journey and be on the lookout for my book. You can find me on all social media platforms and go over to *www. HelenMastanduno.com* to read about my businesses and keep up with my latest accomplishments. I'm Helen Mastanduno, and I want you to know, **you're gonna be big**!

Helen Mastanduno

Helen Mastanduno was born in Ipoh, Perak and grew up in Petaling Jaya, Selangor, Malaysia. She migrated to America on a journey to further her education. During her time in the States, she has gone through many ups, downs, and turnarounds, but she is still standing here, firm,planted, and rising above her circumstances. She holds the firm beliefs that we are created for far more than what we believe and can soar above and beyond what we could ever imagine!

Many don't know where to start or they are just going through hardships right now and can't imagine how they can manage to wiggle their way out of their current circumstances. Despite your struggles, she is here to tell you it's possible and it can happen for you, whatever it is you seek. You must only believe and do the work it takes to get you to the next level. She has almostlost it all and neared bankruptcy at least three times. If she can move forward and into her purpose and obtain success, then you can too!

Mastanduno founded the nonprofit organization Hope and Love, Inc. to aid veteran women and disadvantaged communities. She realized the deficits that veteran women and her surrounding community faced in resources and aid and sought to bridge the gap. She is the President of P.C. Real Estate Firm, Inc. New Jersey Division, and the owner of a branch office.This corporation made history being the first licensed 501(c)(3) real estate corporation in the U.S. Their efforts work hand-in-hand with other branch offices to expand New Jersey's economic development. She also has a cooking show named *Homemade with Helen* on Boss Ladies TV Network.

She wants everyone to know that if you are one that is afraid of taking risks, look at her life as an example of what bravery can bring about. Regardless of how fearful you are, always remember that the acronym of FEAR is False Evidence Appearing Real. Take calculated risks and use wisdom in every decision you make, but never allow fear of the unknown, alone, to hinder you into what possibly could be the life of your dreams.

Helen can be reach at:

instagram.com/helenpkcheong & *PowerfulFemaleImmigrants.com*

FROM SCARCITY TO ABUNDANCE BECAUSE SOMEONE BELIEVED IN ME

Maricela Soberanes, Mexico

I remember entering my boss's office. I stood at the door as he was finishing up a conversation. I didn't want to interrupt him, so I listened attentively and wrote everything he said. I asked him to see my notes when he hung up the phone. He looked at the paper and started laughing. I expressed my desire to learn English. "Can you teach me?" I asked. "I can't help you learn English," he said, still laughing. It felt as if his laugh was stabbing my heart. At that moment, I decided I would learn English and was determined to do whatever it took.

I boarded the bus from Tampico, Mexico, to Austin, Texas, on July 26, 1998, I was 23 years old. It was a long day of travels across the border on a sunny Texas summer. I was traveling alone, carrying a bag with clothes, a few documents, a homemade meal prepared by my mom, and a book a friend gifted me—the overall plan was to learn English.

The driver announced our arrival at our final destination. I quickly gathered my belongings and got off the bus. It was almost nighttime. Before departing from Mexico, I had a phone call with Lety. She was a family member of my coworker and the only person I had as contact in the US. She lived in Austin and kindly said I could stay with her. When I think of this arrangement now, I can see why my mother was worried when we said our goodbyes at the bus station.

I called her as soon as I got off the bus. My heart sank; the line was disconnected. I called the second number she had given me, the restaurant she worked at; it was closed. Alone, scared, and desperate, I got a taxi and found a hotel to sleep in for the night. This nearly exhausted my trip budget; I had no other option.

The following day, I anxiously and excitedly ran towards the window and opened the blinds. I waved at the new world, my new world, "Hello, America!" This was the beginning of my life in America. I made my way to the restaurant; people rushed in for lunch. A smiling face held the door open at the entrance and greeted the customers. Her smile was warm, her eyes bright, and she had a polite voice. As I approached her, I rushed to hug and thank her for letting me stay with her. She looked at me confused and asked, "Table for one?" When I told her I was looking for Letty, she showed me inside and pointed at her.

Letty asked me to wait for her shift to be over and gave me my first meal after over 24 hours. I noticed how busy they were, so I offered to help. The owner handed me a uniform shirt and gave me a minute of orientation, and off I went to help. At the end of the shift, servers came by and gave me money. I looked at Letty, confused; I had no intent to charge for the help. Letty nodded her head, signaling me to accept the tips. This was my first time earning dollars; it was so gratifying. The owner asked me to return; I worked there for over two years.

Often, Letty wanted to take me shopping and show me around the mall. I knew better than to go shopping and spend all my money. The earnings helped pay my share of the bills and, most importantly, send money to my mom for her living expenses. I had promised her that as long as I could work, she never had to again. It was my way to appreciate the years of hard work raising my eight siblings and me as a single mother.

The long bus rides between home and work were the perfect time to study English. With the help of a handheld translator, I translated books, menus, newspapers, and anything I could get my hands on. At the same time, I was trying to register for college. I learned that my business degree from Mexico could not be transferred. To attend college, I needed to start by taking the GED (General Education Degree) exam.

I visited the community college on my days off to get information about college registration. The secretary laughed at me when I tried to explain my situation in my limited English. "How is she expecting to be admitted to college speaking like that?" she told her coworker. I felt like she had punched my stomach; tears filled my eyes as I walked away. I was losing hope. I told myself this was just another door closed, another "no," for now.

Someone told me about free ESL (English as a Second Language) classes; I immediately started attending. There, someone told me about a job helping Spanish-speaking Medicaid applicants submit their applications. Then, nurses would review the applications and assess the patients. That gave me hope that my business experience could be combined with a nursing degree. That became my next goal.

After passing the GED exam, I registered for college courses. During the first semester, I completed the pre-requisite classes for a nursing program (anatomy and psychology, microbiology, statistics, and psychology). All of this while I was still learning English. It was a tedious and slow-moving process. My 3.8 GPA at the end of my first semester felt like a colossal failure. This is because, in Mexico, the grading system is from five (failing) to ten (highest). I was relieved when the counselor explained the grading system in the States; I realized I had a chance at the nursing program.

At the end of that semester, I was able to put my name on the long waiting list to enter the nursing program. The next semester, I was admitted to the nursing program. Finally, I had one foot in the door! At the same time, I lost my roommate and could not pay for the apartment myself; I became homeless for some time.

Living in the United States sounds glamorous to many foreigners. Once here, routine and everyday struggles paint a much different reality. There was nothing glamourous about working and being a student full-time, having little time to rest, or being homeless. Living in the U.S. had its challenges. I missed my family and my friends back home. I lacked community, everyone seemed to be in a hurry, and it was challenging to make meaningful connections. The food was a big shock; even Mexican food differed from what I knew. People seemed to have a lot of material things, and then the unspoken comparison among others. Now I know it's called "keeping up with the Joneses."

Awareness of these cultural differences made me realize I needed to make my new world, instead of adapting to the new world. I focused on keeping a healthy work-school balance. I remained laser-focused on my goals, controlled my money, protected my time, and was very selective about the people I surrounded myself with. I renamed the obstacles in front of me; I called them opportunities.

I used my love for running to add physical activity to my routine. My time on the trail was my way of disconnecting from my hardships and reconnecting with my memories that kept me motivated and encouraged during difficult times.

After graduating from nursing school in 2005, I worked nights at the intensive care unit (ICU). I continued attending school to earn a bachelor's in the science of nursing (BSN). I learned about certified registered nurse anesthesiologist (CRNA), a master's degree entry-level nursing specialty. CRNA schools are demanding; most programs don't allow students to work while attending. I make that my next goal.

While applying for anesthesia school, I needed to obtain my transcripts from the community college. Coincidentally, the secretary who laughed at me years before was who attended me again. In the end, she asked me, "Anything else I could help you with?" I told her, "No, you helped me enough years ago and again today." She said, "Wow, you have a good memory; I don't remember you," I told her what I remembered of the first encounter and how I felt when she laughed at me. Her eyes had tears as she apologized for her actions. I told her, "Believe in others, no matter how different they look or sound. Sometimes, that's all they need."

CRNA programs have a very competitive selection process. I learned later that my first application was among over a hundred others. I was one of the twelve students admitted to the 2009 graduating class.

Even while working as a nurse and paying for full-time college, I saved enough for a down payment to buy a house. The day I got the keys to my home, I became a homeowner and a landlord. I had purchased a duplex; the plan was to live on one side and rent the other. This was an unknown territory. Back in Mexico, our family was so poor that we rented one room to fit a family of ten. The same space was a living room, a kitchen, and a sleeping area. The roof leaked every time it rained; we would take turns emptying the buckets. I talk about growing up in Mexico in my book, *From Scarcity to Abundance*.

Having not only a place to call home but a place to rent and produce income was one of my most significant achievements. About a year into home ownership, I was accepted to anesthesia school. I packed my belongings into a little car and relocated to Memphis, Tennessee. I rented both sides of the duplex, which paid for its expenses. I left, praying that the plan in place worked. Six months later, I received a call from the tenants the roof needed fixing. I hired the wrong contractor, who walked away with my money and left the roof worse off. Fixing it left me with minimal cash reserves for the remaining two years. It was stressful to see the student loan balance grow quickly; I had never borrowed money.

The program was as demanding as expected. Study was all I did, leaving no time for a physical routine. The school stress, lack of physical activity, and worrying about money heavily taxed my well-being. I knew how to find a happy balance, so I resumed running and exercising. I promised myself to prioritize my health above anything else.

I graduated from anesthesia school and started harvesting the rewards of my hard work earning a six-digit salary. Now I could afford to travel to see my mom. We took an extended vacation and had the most memorable time together. That was her first time on an airplane. We both had tears of happiness several times during the trip.

Every day, I woke up with an overwhelming feeling of gratefulness and appreciation for my blessings. I also make it my priority to give back to my community. I committed to doing at least one medical mission yearly, a commitment I continue to fulfill.

Another priority was to take control of my finances. My student loans totaled over $250,000! I worked diligently to pay them back, and I was debt-free sixteen months later. About my goal to achieve the highest degree in my chosen profession, I returned to school and earned a doctorate.

Around that time, I started the process of petitioning for my mother to visit the U.S. We got as far as getting her a passport. Suddenly, she suffered from gastric symptoms. The doctors delivered a terrible diagnosis; it was stomach cancer. In a matter of months, she lost so much weight. She was admitted to the hospital for intravenous nutrition in preparation for surgery. It was devastating to see such a quick downturn in her health. She underwent surgery, and all seemed to have gone well; she never lost her optimistic spirit or bright smile. The surgery was a success! The cancer was removed, and she was discharged to recover at home. While at home, she suffered a surgical complication, and she died on the way to the hospital.

I had to say the most difficult of my goodbyes to my best friend, hero, role model, source of motivation, and biggest cheerleader. Losing her hurt deeper than any other pain I have ever endured. It took away the joy of anything I had or did. I felt as if my purpose in life was lost. There were days I couldn't get out of bed. One night, I dreamt that she was alive, healthy, and happy. I got to say my goodbyes and hugged her one more time. She told me, "Safe travels, go be your absolute best; others need you and appreciate your contributions. Don't worry about me; I will be here waiting for your return." These were the same exact words she told me the first time I left to come to the States.

I knew then I needed to keep going. I woke up early the following day and went for a long run. For every mile I ran, I relived a happy memory I shared with her. I decided to sign up for my first marathon and dedicated the race to her. Running a marathon demands not only training the body but also the mind. As my body gained endurance, my brain gained resilience, clarity, and confidence.

That year, I successfully ran the first of many marathons and earned my doctorate from Baylor College of Medicine. As I walked the stage, for a split second, I saw her in the audience with a big bright smile on her face cheering for me.

Eighteen years after arriving in America, I was a fluent English speaker. I bought and paid in full for a multi-living real estate (RE) property, paid off my student loans, ran a marathon, and performed two medical missions. I was living my version of the American Dream. It was my time to give back to my adopted country. I decided to join the Navy and was commissioned as a naval officer in June 2016.

My family, close friends, and colleagues questioned my decision. Losing my mother caused a true mind shift, putting a higher priority on empowering others. The Navy allowed me to grow personally and professionally while impacting others. The expectation is that as an officer, you are a leader and a mentor to others. I credit my mentors for developing me into the leader I needed to become.

The first time I wore the military uniform, I felt an inundating sense of responsibility to others and a deep connection with others wearing the same uniform. It is incredible how a simple set of clothing can transform you. During my time in the military, I trained with the best, learned valuable life skills, traveled to different countries to serve and practice anesthesia, met amazing people, and had the honor of influencing many lives.

On the RE investing side, I invested in mentorship to learn how to use RE as a vehicle to build wealth. Fast forward three years, I built a rental portfolio comprised of twelve apartments. Then, I met my husband; we grew the portfolio to thirty-five apartments together. Since then, we transitioned to investing in larger multifamily assets. Today, we co-own over 3,000 apartments and other RE assets. We transform communities and employ hundreds of team members. We continue to grow our businesses and continuously challenge our limiting beliefs.

There is no doubt being an immigrant has its challenges. However, immigrant or not, we all face scarcity at some point. These are strategies you can enact to live a life of abundance:

Ask the correct question to the correct person- The quality of questions you ask directly impacts the answers you receive.

The more noise you hear, the more resourceful you must become.

Surround yourself with people who believe in you.

Wealth is a state of mind.

Now, I dedicate my time to helping others become the best version of themselves. I mentor others who were told "no" too many times and lacked resources like me. They can change the world if given the tools to change their own world. You don't know what you don't know until someone believes in you and helps you find the way! I believe in you.

Maricela Soberanes

Maricela is a Certified 10X Certified Business Coach Helping investors to build wealth in Real Estate $270M Portfolio, 3000+ Doors. 16 years of investing, Business Coach, and writer.

Maricela can be reached at:

linktr.ee/upplexrentals and *PowerfulFemaleImmigrants.com*

HARDSHIPS TURNED INTO OPPORTUNITIES

Jazmin Salinas, Mexico

Your hardships, challenges, and barriers will either be the reason why you make it or part of the story you tell when you do make it. And YOU get to make that choice!

My name is Jazmin Salinas. I was born in Mexico into a beautiful family, the oldest of three sisters and a little brother. I was blessed to have a mom that dedicated all her life to raising us, loving us, and being present, but the most important thing that my mom did was pour genuine belief in me. On the other side, my dad taught me all the fundamentals of success, business, investments, ethics, and sacrifices, but the greatest lesson I remember him saying was, "Somebody in the same situation that you are is winning."

A lesson that later on would help me wipe down my tears and keep pushing through life.

When talking about sacrifices, the biggest one of them was migrating to a foreign country. I thought that the immigrant journey started when I was 18 when I moved with my family to the US. But while I was preparing spiritually to write this book, I found out that I had to heal my two-year-old Jazmin. When I was only two years old, my heart was broken when my father had to leave Mexico in search of better opportunities for my mother and I, right after a huge currency crisis that resulted in a recession. While I don't remember much, my mom tells me that I would cry every single day for my dad. I would refuse to eat my meals, arguing it could only be my dad who fed me. I can't even imagine how hard that was for my mom; she was already heartbroken because the love of her life had left without knowing when he would return. On top of that, she knew my dad was facing all the risks of crossing the border while seeing her first and only daughter suffer from the absence of her father.

As for my dad, he was working endless hours to save money for two years. He had a strong purpose and did not stop until he could return to Mexico knowing that every day that he was gone was worth it. He returned two years later to reunite with his family and open a business. Now that I am older, I appreciate all the sacrifices that my parents made.

I grew up so happy. I had it all! My dad instilled in me his entrepreneurial spirit, and I founded my first business at the age of 15. I was a young girl with big dreams and an entrepreneurial heart. Unfortunately or fortunately, my pink bubble exploded when I was 17 years old. My world shattered. My dad got kidnapped by the cartels in Mexico.

Everything I was doing was to make him proud. He was my mentor, my business partner, my motor, the love of my life, my everything.

I remember coming back from college and rushing to get ready for a business gala. As I passed by, I noticed my dad eating alone but didn't take the time to say hi or ask how his day was. It is shocking to think when is the last time you might see your loved ones; I wish I had taken a moment to run into his arms and tell him how much I love him. I was so caught up in my world, that I took my dad's presence for granted.

When I was at the event, my mom called me, and I could tell from the first word she spoke that something was wrong. She sounded like she was trying hard to sound okay, and I could hear the strain in her voice. She simply told me to come back home as soon as I could. When I asked her what had happened, she didn't want to say much, but I could hear her voice breaking.

I could feel her pain even though she was trying to be strong. I rushed back home to witness the saddest scene I had ever imagined. My mom told me that a black Suburban with polarized windows and no license plates pulled up at my dad's business and took him.

A million questions arose in seconds. What should we do? Where can we find him? Who should we call? Should we call the police? What if they are coming back to get us? What if they hurt my dad? At that moment, we decided to surround ourselves with God. We held each other's hands and asked God for compassion and forgiveness because we didn't look for Him when everything was good. Now that we needed a miracle, here we were. A four-year-old child prayed, "Lord, please keep my dad safe and bring him back to us. We need him." An eight-year-old girl said, "Lord, please protect my dad's life and bring him back home." A fourteen-year-old girl prayed for strength and a miracle, while my mother's heart was broken knowing that the love of her life was in the hands of the cartel. And as for me, all I could do was pray for the men who took my dad. Luke 23:34

There are no words to express the suffering in that situation. I remember one day lying on my bed, crying so hard that I felt like I was going to faint. The pain I felt was more than I could bear so I started praying for strength. I never doubted that God was with us and would bring my dad back home, but I felt immensely hurt. At that moment I experienced the Holy Spirit for the first time as I felt like I was in God's arms. He strengthened me. Thirty-four days later my dad came back home. Mark 11:24

Although we were happy and grateful that my dad was back, life wasn't the same. We felt scared and unsafe, never knowing who was watching us. Within a month, my dad decided that we should all move to the USA. He didn't care about leaving his businesses or properties; he just wanted us to be safe and happy again.

Our family of six took a flight to land in Texas. We immediately felt the peace and safety that we had been missing. However, for me, it was overwhelming to continue my education without speaking the language. I also needed a job and a car, and I was heartbroken because I had left my first love back in Mexico. Everything seemed unknown.

When I was in Mexico, I had the opportunity to study at one of the top three universities in the country, Tecnológico de Monterrey. So, I applied to the top universities in Texas. My dad drove me to Baylor University and Texas A&M. First setback, I did not speak English at the time, and as a result, they did not admit me. This left me feeling discouraged and unsure of what to do next. I thought to myself, "What am I going to do here? I don't have a future here. My life and my love are in Mexico." However, my mom was supportive and helped me believe that everything would work out.

Since studying didn't seem like a feasible option, I started looking for a job. However, even to apply, they required a social security number, which involves a lengthy immigration process that can take years. Second setback.

A few months passed and now I was convinced that I needed to go back to Mexico. My dad and my family needed to stay here but I needed to go and get my life back to chase my dreams.

My dad expressed how bad he felt for making me go through this, but he also reminded me that:

"Somebody in the same situation that you are is winning. Jazmin, there has to be a way, you are not the only one. There are millions of immigrants in this country."

SO I WENT AND FOUND MY WAY THROUGH.

I started my first job at a fast-food restaurant, making $7.50 an hour. Although I knew I didn't belong there, I enjoyed being there. It gave me the opportunity to practice and learn English, and I eventually became the best employee at the place. One of my superpowers is to do everything with passion and love. Col 3:23

I was quickly promoted, and a few months later, I started taking business classes at the local community college while working a minimum of 50 hours per week as a manager and being a full-time college student. After tirelessly seeking out opportunities and knocking on doors, I finally understood the logic: while the government wouldn't allow me to work, I could still create businesses and employ people as long as I paid my taxes.

I didn't need opportunities. I had to create them. I didn't need an employer. I needed to employ people. I wasn't allowed to enter corporate America, I had to create corporate America.

My mom did her magic again, unconsciously. She was convinced I could do anything I wanted and sincerely believed I could be a successful businesswoman. Unconsciously, I believed her.

I started doing service audits for businesses as self-employed. CorpAmerica became my client - banks, dealerships, retail stores, and more. After that, I discovered another thing: who doesn't need sales in their business? I sold several businesses in different industries. When you have an entrepreneur mentor at home who you get to call dad, it's hard to blow money or get off track. I had $43k in savings and he said it was time to invest or open a business, but he didn't advise on what or where. So I had to find my way again.

When I started out, I only knew two things for sure: I had no clue what kind of business I wanted to start, and I believed that real estate was the best investment. Within two weeks, I found a piece of land that I liked and submitted an offer for 40k. In the same month, I got the opportunity to sell investment properties for a real estate investment firm. I was fascinated with the real estate industry.

I learned how to analyze properties for investment properties and that knowledge made me realize I did not get a deal on my lot. Fortunately, I was able to sell at a gain of 5k which gave me the confidence and drive to start buying and reselling land lots. As I continued doing land flips, I explored other options in real estate, such as fix and flip, short-term rentals, and fourplexes. I was introduced to Multifamily real estate, and it just made sense to me. Why settle for a fourplex when I could own a building with 100+ units? I realized that owning apartment buildings would allow me to take advantage of tax benefits, generate cash flow, and build long-term wealth. I knew this was the next step for me, so I went all in and found my way into the multifamily real estate industry. Within a year in the multifamily game, I have acquired 880 units and founded the Massive Capital Girls Society. Our society aims to empower successful women to create generational wealth while building meaningful relationships and help, support, and inspire each other to become the best versions of ourselves, growing personally, professionally, and spiritually.

If I can leave you with one thing, it is this: always put God first. I promise you, He will take care of your personal, professional, and spiritual life. There's NOTHING you cannot overcome when you surrender yourself to Him. The eyes through which the world sees you are not the same eyes through which God sees you. For Him, there is no net worth, education level, immigration status, language, or anything else. If He has put a dream in your heart, He will help you break through every single difficulty that the world throws at you.

My challenge was to be an immigrant starting from scratch. I don't know what's yours but what I can tell you is that we all have challenges, and nobody has it together. We have to start where we are with what we have. If you want to make it big, there's no room for you to play the victim role.

"Don't fake it until you make it. Instead, face it until you make it, embrace it, get up, take massive action, and put God first.

Jazmin Salinas

Jazmin is a Serial Entrepreneur at heart, she founded her first start-up and hired her first employee when she was 15, with a broad range of experience working with businesses of all sizes in multiple industries and expertise in customer service and sales, backed up by a couple of business degrees nationally and internationally. 4+ years as an Active Investor in land. Co-Sponsor for 880+ units in Multifamily Real Estate. Founder of Massive Capital Girls Society

Jazmin can be reach at:

Massive.capital/girls-society & *PowerfulFemaleImmigrants.com*

EXCESS BAGGAGE

Jodie Sacco, South Africa

I don't really recall how many days had passed since I'd left my apartment, never mind my room. It was 2018 and the weight of guilt, shame, loss and helplessness was bearing down on me with such a great force, it felt impossible to move. I was pathetic.

Between nonstop bouts of tears, the memories of the amazing life I had had kept playing over and over and over… I used to have everything in the world.

It was all gone. Where did it all go wrong?

As a distraction at some point, I picked up my phone and started mindlessly scrolling through social media.

And there it was.

That proverbial ray of light that suddenly shone into that dark, hopeless cave I felt I was in.

It was a quote that read: "Where focus goes, energy flows." -Tony Robbins

I sat up and said out loud: "This is ALL my fault."

That quote changed everything for me as I realized this: - although I had decided to leave South Africa and to never allow my family to suffer the way I saw them suffer financially and mentally I was still carrying excess baggage. I had left the country of my birth for good, but I had carried with me all the subliminal things that caused a complete nervous breakdown and massive destruction that followed. I was constantly negative in my thoughts, self-talk and outlook on life without realizing it!

My Story of immigration began in April 2007, when we arrived in the US with a suitcase and backpack each. Ironically, America was the last place I ever thought I'd visit, let alone live but you never know where the journey will take you, so being open and unattached to outcomes, I went with the opportunity and of course, the love of my life.

I choose to share my story today, not for sympathy but rather as I mean to impress upon the reader the importance of looking inward when things seem to keep going wrong around you. It's our default, as humans, to blame and try to protect ourselves from being at fault. We all do it until we have that moment of realization. Well, at least I did, and it changed everything.

It's probably the hardest process I ever had to go through - a deep, painful journey of true personal development. The breakthrough came in a moment when I realized I was the common denominator in all that had gone 'wrong' in my life, and it was within my control to change. Sadly, I couldn't remedy all that I had done wrong in the past, but I knew there were others I could truly help from experiencing the same demise. Including our daughters.

I was 17 years old when I recall being overwhelmed with a sense of responsibility beyond my age. This was not something that others 'gave me' but rather a role I chose.

I was raised in a very blue collar, highly religious extended family where I was taught to fear God and live by the words of the bible. I was taught that "money was the root of all evil", "idle hands are the work of the devil" and never, ever leave "the church" or you will be condemned as the black sheep. Rejection became a fear and my first piece of Excess Baggage. I also came to believe that true success was defined by how hard you worked and the sacrifices your family had to make to ascertain that goal, even over weekends and vacations. More Excess baggage.

I also chose to believe that it was my responsibility to change all the suffering and pain I saw around me – not only in my family, but in the people of my Country. You see, I grew up during Apartheid South Africa and vividly recall the separation of white people and people of color.

It bothered me to the extent that I remember being in a small store with my dad where he bought his pack of cigarettes and as I was carefully and slowly choosing which piece of candy I wanted. I noticed a long line of 'Black people' (that's what we referred to African American people as) outside the backdoor of the store. I asked my dad why they were all waiting outside, and he said: "They can't come inside until we leave."

The law prohibited people of color being in the same store as White people, so they had all had to evacuate when we walked in.

I hated it. I didn't understand it and it was confusing to me as a young child.

One of the reasons I even noticed that this was happening around me was because our home was a little different to other families.

Every White home had live-in "servants"; a housekeeper and a Gardener/ Estate Manager. Generally, their living quarters were bare bones and honestly, awful but it was the only way that the African tribal people could make money. They weren't allowed to work in corporate jobs, schools or government.

However, my Mum had grown up in the African Kingdom of Swaziland and in her formative years, had gone to school with mainly African Kids – to the extent that she was the minority as a White kid.

My Dad had been part of the Apartheid police force in his young 20ies and had witnessed the most heinous crimes.

My Dad is a gentle soul so despite his tall and athletic stature, he was traumatized during his early time as an Apartheid Police Office by raiding homes and imprisoning couples who were dating cross racially and seen his fellow police necklaced[1]**** to death in front of him!

My parents just had a different way of being around our staff as a result of their experiences.

Our maid, Gladys and Gardener, Joseph really became an extension of our Family. Gladys cooked for us, babysat and really was a 2nd Mother to my brother and I when both my parents were away from the home working.

Joseph suffered from Polio and was deaf and had a bad leg that he dragged behind him as he walked but we loved him, laughed with him and cared for him like a family member. Each night when the TV programing started, he'd join us in the kitchen to watch whatever was on. They ate the same food as us (although they preferred their

1 The practice of placing a petrol-soaked tyre around the neck of an individual and setting it alight ('necklacing')

staple beans and rice) and we'd help them to send money back to their families in the Townships (the segregated areas where Black people had to live)

I really didn't see 'color' the way many other South Africans did, and it shone a spotlight on the separation in my world outside of home. So that responsibility I felt as a 17-year-old, resulted from wanting to be a part of the change that was so badly needed in our country.

It was around the same time that Nelson Mandela was released from prison too. I became passionate about serving others and volunteered at hospitals, orphanages, and my local junior Council. I was Head Girl of my school, Captain of the Indoor and Outdoor Field Hockey teams, Athletics and Swimming teams and the U16 State Field Hockey Team. Leadership was in my blood and together with this "knowing", I truly believed that I was going to do something very important with my life.

It wasn't until the following year, when I was a Rotary Exchange Student in Brazil, that it finally all came together for me. I needed to become a Diplomat so that I could make a real, positive impact on the lives of ALL South Africans.

I must add though, that my parent's consent and my decision to accept that position in Brazil had us all rejected from our church. Another rejection. More Excess Baggage.

I returned after that incredible year abroad to South Africa and Studied Political Science and Linguistics – The basis for the Diplomatic Civil Servants course. I already spoke Portuguese and was able to add

French and German to the list.

I became more and more excited as I came to the End of my Degree and started planning a move to Johannesburg to be closer to the country's Capital, Pretoria.

And then I got the news. It was my last Political Science Class before final exams and the excitement was tangible. A fellow classmate who was also going the Diplomacy route called me over and I could tell something wasn't right. She broke the news.

"We are not going to be accepted. The Government has instituted all Civil Servant positions as Affirmative Action only." We were both White and hence, *the wrong color.*

My world had been shattered and for a reason that was completely out of my control. I'd been the recipient of the ultimate rejection. I couldn't change the color of my skin.

Ironically, that same week my first ever boyfriend broke up with me over the phone. Another rejection.

The next couple of years passed by with the cloud of Student Loan debt, bad decisions of a 20-year-old and basically a lack of self-care and respect. I had really given up. I defaulted into victim mode. Excess Baggage.

In a small moment of hope, I remembered how my year in Brazil had given me clarity and that traveling and experiencing other cultures brought me joy.

So, I packed my bags and spent 3 months in London and then a year in Taiwan, teaching English.

The whole journey gave me new life and perspective. It was healing to experience the hustle and bustle of London life and the vastly different chaotic culture of the Taiwanese. Despite the language barrier, I totally empathized with their internal conflict of wanting to be independent from China, yet fearful of not having her as their custodian. An identity crisis that became apparent when I joined a peaceful march for independence in Taipei. Another stark fear of rejection was revealed to me.

I returned to South Africa again with an overwhelming sense that I had to be sacrificial in my life for some reason. Again, a great burden of Leadership and responsibility to help others and change lives. This time, I turned my attention to my family though as I had begun to realize how "stuck" many of them were.

I was extremely close to my grandmother, Ruth. We had formed our bond innately but physically through the time I spent with her whilst my Mum and Dad were working as young parents. She was foundational and constant in my life. Until around 16 when I remember noticing a change in her. She became distant… didn't want to do things with me any longer and chose to sit in her chair and stare… another rejection. More Baggage.

From all these experiences still just in my 20ies, I decided to be single and just dedicate myself to my career. That if I had enough money, I could finally support my family – my Grandparents, parents, and brother. I chose to believe that perhaps that was my responsibility of saving my people.

Of course, though, love seems to find its way into our lives when we least expect it. So it was around this time, in 2005 that I met the love of my life. He too was highly independent and had no interest in being married, but our connection was all consuming. Finally - no rejection.

It was a whirlwind of a romance and prosperity and excitement like I had never experienced before personally… only witnessed in my travels through the eyes of the other travelers.

I fell deeply in love and became all consumed.

We had so much fun together and dreamt the biggest dreams. Life became easy, light and so full of passion and excitement. He and his family embraced me and my family in every way possible… life was so good.

He too had traveled extensively and knew the world of opportunities that lay outside of South Africa, so we soon moved to Italy and then the US where we ultimately chose to stay and call it home. That was the year we each arrived with a suitcase and backpack.

People would often stop us and comment on how amazing our energy together was… how we were the perfect couple, and we felt it! Life was so good! The world was our Oyster, and we were living life to the Max!

We both pursued hobbies we were deeply passionate about, built our forever home together and bore two perfect daughters in 2008 and 2010.

I had never felt so complete. His family went above and beyond to take care of me, our girls and my entire extended family. It was so unexpected.

We traveled first class, had an incredible home, amazing friends and family and incredible businesses… but most importantly, we had love.

And so, you ask…. Why on earth did my story start with me being all alone in 2018 in a tiny apartment?

Excess Baggage

Despite all that I had in my relationship, all the love, the material goods, the incredible experiences and help and support from the family I still had the excess baggage.

I carried the baggage from the Church, shame of Apartheid, the rejection from my Nan, affirmative action, the first boyfriend, etc.

And it all culminated in a shocking mindset of lack, fear and flight.

So, at a point in time in our relationship, when my husband was doing a sport that scared me… I was triggered.

When we'd go for a run together and I couldn't keep up with his pace, I was triggered…

When I messed up our finances… I was triggered. I hated failure. I felt like I was letting him down, I felt like I wasn't a good enough mother or wife, and it was all simple because of the fact that I was so negative and didn't see that success was right in front of me!

Rather It was all bundled into one place in my mind: Rejection. I am being rejected again! Now this wasn't his fault. This was 100% all my 'stuff' and this excessive excess luggage that I had never dealt with, suddenly bore down on me and I cracked.

As humans, when we are under extreme pressure we go into fight or flight mode and it's a place where no logic or reasoning exists.

So that is what I did. I ran away from it all and boy! Did I fight. All I did was create a path of destruction that caused a gigantic, deeply painful heartache, embarrassment and shock. In those moments, I didn't feel, I just felt like I existed and honestly, hardly recall the decisions I was making or the things I was doing.

I ran away from all that was good in my life. All that was supportive and accepting and full of prosperity because despite leaving the country of my birth with just that suitcase and backpack, the excess baggage I carried was invisible yet all consuming.

I took full responsibility at that moment in 2018 as I mindlessly scrolled through social media and found that quote.

I know, you think I am blaming my actions and bad decisions on my past (excess baggage), but this is this point: I don't blame it, I take ownership of it. It's mine and I finally see it and carry it and know how to offload it, unpack it and store what is needed but discard that which no longer serves me.

For the past several years I have dedicated myself to self-education - a longing to understand how I destroyed the only true authentic love I had and the opportunity I was blessed with to change my family and my people's lives, especially with all the amazing opportunities we have in the US. I spent hours and thousands of Dollars on education, coaching and mentoring to understand what happened and where I went wrong, the answer still amazes me.

Choices.

We all have choices…. Despite. That's right. It doesn't matter what has happened in our lives. How many times you were rejected, overlooked, rejected again…. There is always a choice. We can decide to live our lives from a glass half empty, or a glass half full. Our past does not define us.

The Choice I made that day when that life-saving quote came up on my newsfeed was this: I cannot undo what has happened, I can only control what I do moving forward.

I decided that all that had happened was really for a reason bigger than myself and that from that day onwards, I would use my mistakes to help our girls and others not make the same ones.

I initially thought of being a Mindset coach, but it didn't seem that it would make a big enough impact in the lives I wanted to affect. So, I chose to rather go the Business Consulting route where I knew I could use my experience of starting and growing businesses as well as support the Business owner on breaking through any limiting self-beliefs from their own excess baggage.

I moved into coaching when I joined a Network marketing business where I quickly became a top earner, and I realized that Business Coaching was where I wanted to be.

Today, I am a certified Business and Executive Coach and have successfully coached business owners to grow and scale their companies by as much as 176% in just 90 days. I truly love what I do because I can see the greater impact these types of results have on businesses, the owners, the staff, all their families and the communities they are in.

It gives me no greater joy than to hear a business owner say they have broken through a mindset barrier and as a result, their income has increased or that they have implemented systems and processes that allow them more free time to spend with their families.

And then there are the lessons I have learnt and continue to learn each day. For this I thank our precious Daughters for always keeping me honest and accountable. Because of them, I chose to become a better version of myself each day as they are my priority and I will never, ever allow anything to change that. We openly talk about our goals and dreams, and they support me in my journey of rebuilding and healing by serving others to be successful in their goals and dreams.

It's funny to me now how my positive mindset shift has rubbed off on them as I often hear them saying positive phrases of affirmation or see them making decisions to leave a friend group because of a certain negativity. The girls are also huge philanthropists at heart, and I believe this is because of the role modeling they learn from their family and me. They are always trying to feed the homeless on the street corner and discuss ways they can build a shelter for the Mentally Ill.

Choices. Whether they are good or bad ones, never, ever underestimate the far-reaching effect yours will make on others. I would urge each one of you to check in with yourself. Do you have excess baggage that causes you to make bad choices? Do you feel that bad things just keep happening to you? Is your business failing again? Is your marriage under pressure?

Please don't leave that excess baggage unpacked. It will eventually be too heavy to bear.

Here are my top 4 lessons I'd love to impart:

1. Everyone has bad things happen to them. We all get a choice to decide how we respond in that situation: - Be the victim or rise above and be the victor. Being the victim will cause excess baggage.
2. As Humans, it's our default to blame people or circumstances around us as the reason for bad things happening to us - We should rather always look to ourselves to blame first.

3. You, your business, your goals and dreams etc. can never grow beyond your own in competencies. Always invest in your own self-development first and then everything else around will flourish as you do.

4. Never underestimate how deeply others around you are affected by the simple choices you are making daily. By getting rid of excess baggage, your ability to make better choices will dramatically improve.

If you want to learn more about how you can work with Jodie, please visit: jodiesacco.com or follow her on all social media at @ jodiesacco

---

Jodie Sacco

Jodie Sacco is an Experienced Entrepreneur, Business Owner, Leader, Public Speaker, Certified Business Coach, Certified Executive Coach and a proud Board Member of Make-A-Wish® Southern Nevada.

Jodie has experience in all areas of business from starting as an entry-level employee to C suite Leadership, including team training, sales, Marketing, Operations & team synergy. Her drive is linked to her Vision to be of service and uplift communities through Business re-education as a Coach, Mentor and Philanthropist.

Jodie obtained her bachelor's degree focused on Political Science and Linguistics from University of KwaZulu-Natal / University of Natal, South Africa. Currently residing in the USA. She has lived on 5 Continents & speaks 5 languages. This has given her a global understanding of diversity, inclusion and challenges that could be linked to cultural backgrounds. Constant student of Personal Development and a Wanderluster of this world.

Jodie knows rejection, failure and adversity. More importantly, she knows resilience.

A life-long athlete who is highly competitive and believes that coming in 2nd, is never an option. As a result, she is fierce in her pursuit of success for her clients although friends know her to be kind, patient, empathetic & fun, especially when she says American phrases with her 'funny' accent!

If you, like Jodie, are committed to excelling and only being Number 1, reach out to Jodie to learn how to work with her.

Jodie can be reach at:

JodieSacco.com & *PowerfulFemaleImmigrants.com*

BLESSED TO BE A BLESSING!

Suzen Zachariah, India

I was born in Kerala, India and went through the educational system in my surrounding district. I lived with my parents all throughout my schooling. I was very close to them; especially with my mother. Ever since I was young, my mother always told me to pray for a good family and future, and so I did ever since I was in elementary school.

I studied for a career in pharmacy, and after I graduated, I had the opportunity to come to the United States. I arrived in New York in 2002. Although I had completed my training and was a licensed pharmacist in India, I still had to pass certain tests here in the U.S. before I could work as a pharmacist here. This was absolutely fine to me as I understood the importance of prescreening and qualifying healthcare workers. However, what I did not expect was the complexity and challenge of comprehending the way these tests were designed. I had completed all my schooling and was fluent in English growing up. However, the dialect in America is different than in India. In school, we had learned more of "British English" and it was initially a challenge to understand the English spoken in America. The testing was somewhat of an obstacle. In my earlier studies, much of it was based on memorization and choosing the best answer, however the tests I took in the U.S. were more based on "choose the best answer".

After passing my pharmacy exams, I remember I had to do 1 year of internship as a pharmacy technician before I could be a pharmacist. The hourly pay at that time was $5.25/hour. At this wage, it was very challenging to meet the living conditions in New York. I fortunately was able to complete my internship and become a pharmacist. I had worked for a national chain pharmacy at that time which directed me to work at various stores in the tri-state area. I remember driving a 20 year old used car with 150K miles on it across the bridge from New York to New Jersey in the cold snowy winters. My husband and I went through many financial struggles and when my son was 2 years old, we decided to move from New York.

We arrived in Dallas, TX in 2008 with very little funds and resources. My husband and I were both working for corporate America and so therefore were able to transfer our jobs from New York to Texas. For us, we knew that we did not want to work in the corporate world for the rest of our life. We understand that many public companies need to work in the best interest of their shareholders and not so much for their employees. I remember in 2008, when the economy was not doing well, many companies, including ours, had cut employee 401K plans just so that they could keep the stock price high on Wall Street.

In 2010, we had the opportunity to leave our jobs and acquired a small pharmacy. It was a huge challenge for us because we did not know how to run a business, nevertheless a pharmacy. The owner was selling it because he did not know how to operate it and was losing $10K a month. This made it an even more risky venture. However, we prayed about it and felt that the Lord was leading us to this venture. We saved up all we had, borrowed from our 401K, took out an SBA loan, and finally acquired the pharmacy in 2011. I remember the pharmacy was a 600 sq ft space with very limited business. I started working there and managed the pharmacy while my husband assisted in marketing to the nearby medical offices. It was initially a very rough and stressful period as we counted every dollar coming and watching every dollar leave our bank account. However, we continued to preserve. We had faith that God was going to elevate us regardless of the current business conditions.

After two years, the business started doing well. We were growing and we moved out of the small space and moved into a 3000 sq space nearby. We expanded from dispensing just prescription medications to compounding. Then in 2016, we had the opportunity to take over another suite in the building and build out a home infusion pharmacy. Then a medical clinical. We went from having 1 employee to several dozen employees at one time. During this process, I learned how to become a prominent pharmacy and also a cutting edge business woman. I learned about the financial aspects of operating a company. I learned how to hire, train, and build a team of people. I learned the insights of business that would help me make the best decisions for the company. I noticed that we were such an influential business that we had patients driving from different cities and towns 40+ miles away, passing by 8-9 other pharmacies, just to come get their medications from us.

In 2019, I was blessed to have the opportunity to build my house in Westlake, TX. I immediately took the initiative to design the layout prior to construction. The timeline to custom build a house takes about 18 months, and I was very involved in every aspect. I did not know that I had an eye for interior design until I started selecting paint colors, furniture, and decorative items.

Our journey has been a blessing. We saw the hand of God guide me from my early stage in life to where I am today. The most joyous endeavor that I took on is our involvement in charity and ministry work. My husband and I both have a heart for children enslaved in human trafficking. We are big supporters of this fight. In 2017, we traveled to the country of Nepal, and stayed at an orphanage with multitudes of children who were rescued from human trafficking. In that part of the world, there are very few luxuries. The children in the orphanage do not have many choices for food and many times they eat what they grow. They do not have the latest iphones or ipads. I remember asking the missionaries what we should bring the children from the USA, and he said the children would love to have chocolate. Thus, we brought them chocolate and handed them out. It brought tears to my eyes because it was like Christmas for them!

As God continues to elevate my family, we look forward to many missionary trips to help many of the people around the world. I believe that we are blessed to be a blessing to others.

Suzen Zachariah

Suzen Zachariah has been in the pharmacy industry for over two decades. She is an experienced Pharmacist and a successful business Owner. She has started and operated multiple businesses while fulfilling her role as wife and mother to two children; ages 13 and 17. She also plays an active role. alongside her husband, in building a real estate investment fund that helps passive investors earn a double digit return. Suzen has a heart to help others. Thus, she loves connecting with people. Suzen is active in her church and arranging fellowship gatherings in her home. Suzen has embarked on missions work throughout the world, and is continuously looking to help others make an impact in the world. She and her husband of 21 years, find joy and fulfillment in spending time with family.

Suzen can be reach at:

linktr.ee/suzen.z & *PowerfulFemaleImmigrants.com*

STRONG - BRAVE - UNBREAKABLE

Izabel Parreira, Brazil

First Five Years

Leaving Brazil, the country of so much color, energy, delicious food, different culture, four seasons and natural beauty, was never my goal. After completing my university degree I quickly realized that it would take a lifetime for me to achieve my dreams and I decided to try my chance and move to America.

One month before the tragedy of September 11, I arrived in NYC for an AU Pair training. I spent one year working in Michigan and Maryland as an AuPair. My host mother corrected almost every word I said, and although it was uncomfortable, she was an essential part of me learning a second language and for that I am grateful. Less than a year after arriving in the US I fell in love and got married. Our love story only lasted for 18 months and we decided it was better for us to go our separate ways. What followed was a very difficult time for me; for the first time I was really alone, away from my parents, away from my host family, separated from my spouse and not knowing which way my life was going. I lost a lot of weight and didn!t know how I was going to make it.

In my next professional chapter, I worked as office manager for an insurance company. I was blessed to meet a great woman from South Africa who was my supervisor and quickly became a mentor and friend. This experience was a decisive turning point in my life. My strong nature was slowly coming back. I made many new friends and eventually at church I met Paulo, a wonderful caring man. While we were dating I suffered an accident and he cared for me with a lot of love. Our connection grew deeper during that difficult time, and I knew he was the one I could share my life with.

From Hustling to Broken Bone to Marriage to Biggest Loss

Before meeting Paulo, I was working three jobs, my time was consumed and I wanted to learn as much as I could. Growing and learning have always been my goal. I had a corporate job during the day and at night did tax returns and worked for a high luxury brand in the Galleria. During the second year of doing tax returns I met another influential person whom I deeply admired for his knowledge and wisdom. He kindly started teaching me the secrets of real estate investments. We became Investor partners and went to a lot of Real estate events. We invested together in the Dave Lindahl program, went to his Bootcamp in the Bahamas and went to M5 Summit in Orlando. Although I didn!t understand everything I was exposed to, this was a very intense learning period for me. After reading Robert Kiyosaki's book Rich dad poor dad, I was eager to invest right away no matter what. In 2006 I purchased my first property and renovated myself with the help of a few friends.

By the end of the year my business partner and I had put a few offers on properties, but none went through. I was, however, able to rent one room in my condo for rental income. I started studying at night with BOMI International to get the Property Management Certification. At that time I was working in Washington DC and the real estate investment with my partner was put in pause mode due to the big market crash.

On Independence day of 2008 while riding my bicycle I fell on the concrete sidewalk and broke my femur. Paulo(still my boyfriend at the time) stood by my side, put a pause on work and cared for me. I was immobilized for four months and worried about the future again. What got me through this difficult time was the love and care from my mother and Paulo.

The following year I received a call from a road patrol officer asking questions about my real estate partner. He had gotten into an accident driving back to Virginia from Pennsylvania. My number was the last one called on his cell phone. Sadly his life ended that day and I could not see my future in real estate without him.

My father's visit to the US was for my wedding in the summer of 2009. It was a fantastic and magical time, I continued to work in my corporate job and taking Property Management courses. On the weekends I was dedicated to my parents, showing them around and doing short trips which my father really enjoyed. Just before he returned to Brazil he began to talk about pain in his stomach, but refused to go to a doctor. Soon after his arrival back in Brazil, the doctors diagnosed that he had stomach cancer and gave him a few months to live. He immediately got admitted in a specialized treatment center a couple hundred miles from home. I booked a trip and stayed there a few weeks, returned to visit during Christmas holiday and then again in February when he passed away during that visit.

I have a horrible mixed feeling of pain and guilt that the night before he passed I talked to God and said something like this:

"Heavenly Father, you have seen how much of a positive, happy, funny and with an enormous heart this man that worked since eight years old is, this man that never failed to provide for his family, that sacrificed his health working long hours away from home. Oh Lord I plead you to not let him suffer anymore, his joy of living has left him long ago, he feels miserable, although he does not say it, we all know that he feels disgusted with his own body, especially from being a person that always praised and cared to be well trimmed, dear God, please operate a miracle in his body that is now only bone, but if you can't have him healthy Lord please take him away and end his agony."

A Miracle and an 'A-ha' Moment!

Fast forward to June 2016. After years of trying to get pregnant, going through fertility treatment and many negative results I gave birth to my son. I'm often asked do you have only one? My answer is a resounding: "**No, I have everything!** He is the much expected baby, the result of many nights awake, many tears, and the answer to many prayers. I am blessed and happy beyond belief each day for the courage and energy he gives me to keep on facing life's challenges head on and not give up.

Covid came, I was laid off, and realized that **I(big I) had the control and could myself** write my own story. I wanted to take control of my life, I wanted to watch my son growing up and be present for him, I wanted to help change people!s lives and create an impact for a bigger purpose. I did a bit of soul searching and knew I didn!t want to invest anymore of my most valuable gift (time) building somebody else!s dream, I received a couple of job offers, but opted not to take them.

I rediscovered my passion and after 4 months, formed a real estate company, given a whole new perspective seeing the opportunity to give it another try. I knew that no matter what happened I was not going to give up or stop until my goals were achieved in balance with my passion for family and community. I've harnessed my energy and enthusiasm to work even smarter and harder than before dedicating long hours, reading, studying, attending courses, webinars, doing property flips, investing in syndications, and joint ventures to build on my now mature acumen and understanding of the business.

Along with forming my company in January 2021 I went back to work with the sole goal to invest the earnings in Real Estate. It was a very busy and productive year, which made me truly excited through each win.

Along with five ladies I partnered to do flips. We met via Zoom regularly, in person a few times and we celebrated each win, in September we put the last touch in our first house on the market. In October I invested in 320 units, as my first multifamily syndication located in Dallas. In the next year I invested in seven more properties. I truly value the experience of these deals, properties and operators. The distributions showed me that there is no get rich quick and that investments are built up over time.

At the end of 2021, we each got Covid at separate times at home and each time had to quarantine. The light bulb went on for my husband that we should move to Florida. We kept on praying for answers and that God!s will would be done.

My husband's helper quitting and my husband!s suffered injury in the Spring coupled with locating a good off market house in Florida were strong signs that we should move. I called my mother to travel from Brazil to help us pack and move, sold my first rental property, gave notice at my job and in June of 2022 my husband went to our new house to demo and start renovation. At the end of the month I drove 17 hours, with my mother and son to our new place leaving 21 years of Washington DC metropolitan area friends, brothers and sisters in Christ, I bring forward 16 years of Property Management career. And am grateful for my husband willingness to leave his 15 years as a licensed class A general contractor and wonderful clients to rebuild a new practiced business in Florida.

Starting All Over

The first six months living in Florida trying to re-establish ourselves, I consider as the hardest time of my life, that lonely road of entrepreneurship hit pretty hard… I never thought I wanted to be an entrepreneur because is having the responsibility to run the hamster wheel 24/7 to get ahead….But the beginning of building your empire while investing in assets to provide cash flow takes time and consistency. It may look glamorous from the outside, but if you are not strong and determined you fall. I believe however, that now nine months later I have found myself to be more resilient.

Joining a multifamily mentorship group focused on mindset and abundance, studying financial education to become a licensed consultant and mainly my daily commitment to prayer with gratitude approach helped me see the light at the end of the tunnel, better yet, see that I can be the light, these reminded me that I choose and I have the power.

Remembering the fact that took me 10 years to realize what my father was trying to tell me means I can't go back to that life, I owe it to him, to my son, my husband and my mother and above all to myself to be the best version of myself which I know I have all qualities and can be strong, loving and always very determined.

Besides the difficulties I have always considered myself blessed to have always had basic needs covered. I was able to move to a country where I did not speak the language, I did not know the rules, I did not know how to drive more than from home to school, I did not know anyone, I did not have family or any friends waiting for me.

I moved to a strangers house(host families), then alone again when separated. I learned to pay my bills, buy a house and be completely independent. I used to be annoyed to hear people asking all the time when I simply introduced myself, where are you from?" because it made me feel excluded, not belonging, being judged by my thick accent…that was one of hardest challenges I had to overcome. Lately I have, however, been owning it. I am proud to be an immigrant. I know I am strong and brave to cross the ocean, learn a new language, a new culture and constantly be out of my comfort zone to build time and financial freedom.

I am immensely in love with this country. From the very first year, friends commented that I was already americanized, or more American than Brazilian, because I was so focused on work. I am thankful for this country to have received me and for the many people that have embraced me simply the way I am, recognizing that I am stronger than I give credit to myself.

Overcoming Fear

After two years of therapy and seeing a doctor early in 2023 I was diagnosed with ADHD. I search for the best tools to navigate this, and the best possible way for myself to live in peace with my body and brain and live a healthier and more balanced lifestyle.

One year ago, I was able to tell my therapist something very personal that I'd kept as a dark secret since I was twelve years old. In my innocence, fear, and trauma I did not know that keeping a sexual abuse I suffered hidden from everyone was going to create so many personal issues in my life such as trust and self confidence. I was really shocked that someone so close to me could do this, and I didn!t know if it was normal.

Throughout my life I had the overwhelming feeling of inadequacy, fear of being criticized paralyzed me, these created self-doubt and made me feel lost and unable to see my gifts, worth, and values for a lifetime.

We have just scratched the surface, there is a lot of work that needs to be done to fix 35 years of trauma, but I am more than ready for treatment and to see the many things that happened throughout my life can now be explained.

Today I see that I can write my own story, I am the driver of it, I am more than enough, after all **I am the daughter of the King**! After much trial and error on my path to success, I realize I can be the best version of myself when I give priority to the Lord and reflect on my inner health before focusing on busy and loud work that the world does not stop throwing at us.

The thought "I would have loved an overnight success" crossed my mind, but my reality has been so different, nothing has been easy or handed down to me, every single thing I am and I conquered, as little as it is, I got through, blood, sweat and tears,. I want to tell you, dear Reader, don't give up! Make a choice to believe, a choice to live your best life now, think of Fear as Feeling Excited And Ready, and go for it, I believe in you!

Recently I was speaking and was asked two questions: 1- "How come you are not afraid" and 2- "What do you want to accomplish in life". My answers were: I am afraid, I just choose to not be the victim of the circumstances, I can and did change them and turned them in opportunities to grow and that is my main goal to help others understand the value of money, that money should not be spent to impulsively buy things to "keep up with the Joneses", but to first invest into something that will give them return, be it financial education, or put money away to gather and purchase an investment property, not a primary home. My goal is to help people understand that when they invest their money in financial education and real estate, they are basically buying their freedom early, and the sooner they invest the sooner they will reap the benefits while healthy, young and alive. Happiness is to enjoy life with whatever you choose that will give you fulfillment however, in order to do that you owe it to yourself to work smarter and to your family to cover and protect them from life's unexpected circumstances, by covering themselves with tools and strategies to help them get there faster. This is my passion and what I teach as a licensed consultant, you can learn more details by going into my social media and/or scheduling a time in my calendar.

When I was called to write the chapter I was surprised and thought, I have not arrived, I am not where I want to be, much less where society expects, but I feel honored to have been invited to be part of this revolution of many powerful immigrant women standing up to tell their own story and for that I &2 grateful! I believe in hard work, just like my father had, and many here share. I believe that team work does make the dream work! I might not be "there" Yet, but I am 100% grateful for my journey because it polished me to be strong, resilient and a powerful (immigrant) woman.

I feel this is just the beginning of a new chapter in my life full of wins, new discoveries, challenges and blessings. I want to be the best version of myself for myself and make my son proud. I am leaving the heaviness and the darkness behind and seeing the beautiful path of newness, of uniqueness for the gift each day brings us, another opportunity. I want to inspire kids, teens, men and especially women to believe they can do anything they set their mind to do, as long as it!s pure, honest, edifying! I want to create impact and inspire a life worth living. I don!t want to simply be alive, I want to shake things up, and make my life and people's life go from survive to thrive! If I can change the life of at least one person through this book I will be very pleased.

Regardless of where you are, if you have reached your dreams or not. If you are selling food in the streets or a high paid executive, never stop having goals and never stop believing in you because God has not and you are wonderfully made by him. There is no comparison, because only you can write your own story, like your fingerprint you are unique, strong, powerful!

Dear reader, my information is below and I would be glad to hear from you, please feel free to reach out and get connected.

Psalm 23 is my favorite

Izabel Parreira

Property Management — LEED Green Associate — Real Estate Investor

The passion about space transformation, repurposing and community impact created and achieved by Real Estate industry, easily translated into Izabel becoming a real estate investor.

For the last 16 years she worked as a Commercial Property Manager prioritizing integrity and collaboration as key success factors in growth. She graduated in Business Administration and received an associate degree in accounting leaning on these foundational skill setsto realize cost-effective, strategic opportunities. Her drive for continued improvement naturally provided personal genuine care for each client by delivering professional, timely and accurate financials leaving each property in a better state than found therefore increasing their value.

Her first real estate investment saw a 33% ROI. Second one was a Single Family Home that was totally renovated mainly by herself and husband labor's then rented. She partnered with PowerHouse Women Real Estate Investing for flip projects and in late 2021 started investing in Multifamily syndications and short term rental Joint ventures.

She is a part of an asset management team for a 200-units storage facility in Fort Piece, where she is also working to develop affordable homes. Her investment portfolio consists of Residential Multifamily in seven states with over 1,000 units; a retail shopping center in Maryland of 68 units in 437,079 SF and a couple of lots inFlorida.

One of Izabel's goals as an immigrant and forever student, is to help bring financial awareness and education to the latino community. Another one is to continue sponsoring charity organizations by increasing financial contributions to causes similar to what was done with WV contributing monthly by adopting kids and availability of time and money to do volunteer work at church, and underserved communities. She is one of the proud founding members of the PH Women Giving Group which support humanitariancauses.

Real estate training, bootcamps, and investing groups: David Lindahl, M5-Five Million Net Worth, Women's Real Estate Investment Network, Earn as you Learn with Higher Point Investing, Grant Cardone Real Estate Summit, founding member of Powerhouse Group Flips. Currently member of Alex Love Li's - Legends General Partnermentorship.

Izabel can be reach at:

izabelparreira.com & *PowerfulFemaleImmigrants.com*

HOW I UNLOCKED MY TRUE SELF

IN THIS NEW WORLD TO UNLOCK AND UNLEASH THE POWER IN OTHERS

Shirley Baez, Dominican Republic

I was born in Quisqueya La Bella, Dominican Republic where you have lush greenery and white sandy beaches, sounds like paradise, right? It is, but for this little native girl growing up in this beautiful Island, it wasn't all paradise. You see my parents, wanting to the American Dream immigrated to the United States and left me behind. I was first with my Godmother (on my mother's side), she was so very loving and caring. She had two sons, they were both night and day; one was ambitious and an exceptional student, the other, the black sheep.

Unfortunately, I remember most of my time having to deal and be in the path of the black sheep of the family, enduring verbal and physical abuses. On top of that the yearning I had for my mother. She would come from time to time to visit me. It was exhilarating when she came as I feverishly anticipated her arrival. We laughed, hugged and exchanged mother and daughterly love, but when it was time to go, it was like my whole world would come down on me. It was very emotional for me, to compensate for her not being with me and to have some remanence of her, I kept a piece of clothing which I smelled to remind me of her essence.

I remember my Godmother not being able to take care of me anymore because of her ill mother, so I was then transferred over to my grandfather (My Dad side) where in his house lived my aunt and kids and her husband. That wasn't a walk in the park either. I felt neglect and abandonment as my aunt only paid attention to her children. I think my parent thought that everything was fine, but in all actuality I was not, I had contacted the mumps and was full of lice. Again, I don't think my parents knew to the fullest what was really going on with me although I'm sure they knew something was wrong because one day, I saw my savior come to rescue me, My aunt, Carmen. After that, my life changed. She rid me of my lice and mumps and brought me here on a one-way ticket to freedom!

Coming to the United States and adjusting to the customs was no easy task. New country, new language, new way of doing things, but also new possibilities! I was so awe struck at the high skyscrapers, the people, the snow! I remember thinking one time, "where is the snow coming from"? "I thought that people were throwing it from the apartments above that I went ahead to the freezer and got ice cubes and started throwing it out the window! LOL. Because Of my naivete and lack of the language, I also got in trouble at school.

One anecdote that I remember was at school, at the time I still didn't know English, but somehow, I ended up in a bilingual class with my teacher primarily speaking English. I remember I was in 3rd grade. We were all at lunch and before we all went back to class, the principal wanted to address all of us. I remember him scolding us and then all I can remember him saying was "and who wants to go to detention" I automatically raised my hand because I understood him saying something else (Me and my limited understanding of the English language) sent me straight to detention where I spent the rest of the day. I never raised my hand again, until I better understood the language. I think about those things now and laugh so hard.

But there was also a dark side, a side that growing up in New York, I had become adrift at sea, feeling lost, confused, and directionless. I came to the realization that I no longer had a nuclear family. My dad and mom had gotten divorced; and so, I did not have two parents to guide and encourage me. My dad worked many hours trying to survive and make ends meet, so I only saw him every other weekend, and my mom whom I lived with was practically absent for most of my young life. She struggled with gambling addiction which I came to soon find out when I lived with her. I had to grow up quickly, take care of myself, and go at it alone, not having somebody I could emulate to build the foundation of becoming a confident and successful young lady. I was lost in this brick city where it felt cold, dangerous and hostile. I didn't know where I was, I didn't truly know myself and where I was heading.

For years, I struggled to find myself and my path. I got into abusive relationships, which further diminished my self-esteem. Since I was a young girl, I was always very creative and involved in many activities that nourished those talents; however, I didn't have the role model I needed to encourage and cheer me on, providing me with guidance so I could keep pursuing what I loved. I dropped out of high school due to not having a supporting structure, a loving household that would support my endeavors and creativity.

I hung out with the wrong crowd often in places that I wasn't supposed to and exposed to things that were unhealthy for me. All of this led me toward an abusive relationship further degrading me mentally, emotionally, and physically; that's when I hit rock bottom. But I knew something was out there; I knew there was much more to life than what I was living. I always believed that your environment determines where we go in life; its significantly difficult to change ourselves and our lives, without changing our environment.

I decided I needed to change and change my environment, so I went to register for college and see if I was eligible for a grant. My credentials were returned as unqualified for grants because my dad made too much money; even though I didn't live with him then. Feeling defeated, I walked back through the train station. There, I saw this big kiosk and sign saying, "We'll pay for your college." I knew that was my calling; I knew that was my sign for yet again a great opportunity.

It happened to be a kiosk to join the U.S. Military. That was precisely the calling I was looking for, and that's when I decided to join the United States Army. Around this time, terrorists struck the twin towers in downtown New York City. I remember thinking two things: "What in the world did I get myself into" and "I am making a vow to serve for the country that provided me a second chance at a great life" From that point, I was committed to a path toward service.

I had gained my purpose at that moment; although I still didn't know where I was heading, what I was doing, where I was going, I was committed to the what the outcome would be. You see, as you try to change your environment whether it is physical or mental, these uncertainties play tricks in our minds, like witches trying to cast spells on our sanity and the massive decisions we try to make. Those were the same questions ruminating in my mind as I decided to change the course of my life.

Although I was unhappy where I was in life before the military, it was still familiar territory, it was all I knew. However, I couldn't shake off the feeling of wanting to pursue the path of higher learning and higher purpose. I needed to think creatively to achieve the right path in my life and start guiding myself toward a better future.

I know that for many young women living in a new country, a bustling city, not having a parent or good role model or resources to support and encourage you can be challenging. Lacking support and still in the developing phase in their lives, they have no choice but to figure it out alone, to figure out who they are, what to do, and want to be when they grow up.

But here I am and there I was, ready to move forward. For a lot of us, we know that we need to leave situations that do not fit us, that do not make us better people. We need to leave environments and situations that are not serving but destroying our creativity, decrepitating us because we're not being exposed to an environment that provides us the opportunity to grow and be the best versions of ourselves.

I started to build my career in the military. For me, this environment challenged me in so many ways and began molding me to be the leader I am today. I was placed in situations where my mental and physical abilities were challenged daily. To conduct obstacle courses, to go to the range to use a weapon and shoot a target to see if I could hit the objective, to learn how to medicate and provide life savings techniques to an injured individual took a lot of practice, and it was very scary, but I still went ahead and did it. Sometimes, we were put in situations where we had no choice, that's where we excelled the most. Whatever you choose as your environment; to explore what you're made of and what you can do is going to be scary…. STILL DO IT ANYWAY, that was always my motto.

I climbed through the ranks very quickly because again, I had found an environment that nourished my qualities and abilities as a human, as woman, as a powerful immigrant woman. Many times, I was recognized for my accomplishments and even surpassed a lot of my colleagues. I took on many leadership roles as I led, cared, and mentored others on their growth as leaders. I took this responsibility very seriously not only because of the nature of our Job, but most importantly I had learned how to discover who I was in this country and environment despite my upbringings and my past situation. Most importantly, I gravitated towards my powers and thus learned how to lead myself first.

All these great things came at a cost however because of the male dominated environment I was in. first because I was a woman and deemed "weaker" and second because I am a minority thus people labeling and stereotyping you; there was bound to be challenges. How did I deal with these challenges you might ask?

I gravitated towards my powers and learned how to lead myself first. You see, when you figure that out, you attain confidence and thus attain the confidence of those who choose to follow you. Now, my Soldiers were looking to me for leadership and guidance and I was happy to mold them into the leader they were about to become. When I started tapping into my powers, everything around me began to shift to my benefit. Everybody began to respond differently; the work I was doing was more polished and purposeful. I knew that I was meant to provide to the world.

We must show up and show out. We are powerful and audacious women, the queens of our thrones. We must embrace our gifts, understand that we are so much more, and can take over challenges. We need to be honest with ourselves and secure in our skin, which only sheds when leveling up. Once I began knowing my powers and providing my gifts to the world, I started to scale up the ranks.

I was more self-aware, cognizant of what I was doing, and through my initiation of lifelong self-development and self-improvement, I could lead myself in a healthy way. I wasn't afraid to take charge, speak in public, voice my opinion for fear of not being liked or judged, or make decisions about what was best for my soldiers and the organization. I didn't come to that point haphazardly; I had to do the work and toil through my internal demons and feelings of inadequacy because of abandonment issues so that I could shed that dead skin and forge forward toward new horizons.

I became one of the few high ranking minority women leaders in an elite community called "Special Operations Forces". As my career started ending in the Military. I noticed that as I transitioned, people still looked to me for leadership, mentoring, coaching, and being an inspiration in their lives. I knew then that I had the responsibility to help others lead well and adjust their mindset to live up to their fullest potential.

According to an CNBC article, more than half (58%) of women under 30 say that career advancement and professional development opportunities are more important to them over the past two years. Professional working women understand the importance of "having a seat at the table matters and are more willing to ask for it."

"But while women aspire to senior management positions as much as their male colleagues, the report found they are far more likely to experience microaggressions that undermine their authority and discourage their ability to advance within a company." I want to change that.

With my love for coaching and mentoring, I created The LeadHERrship Academy which I am the proud founder and CEO of. LeadHERship Academy is a company that empowers professional women to step into their power and captain their professional and personal lives as true bosses. I see that a lot of women either quit their jobs or prefer to stand on the sidelines while their male counterpart make it through the ranks because they are afraid or get frustrated at the fact that they won't have the same opportunities to advance in their field. My passion for this subject also inspired me to become a speaker and a published author of the book " Lead Your Ship, unlock your true self, and Captain your ship like a boss."

All in all, there's no such thing as setbacks, only lessons learned. Now it's time to be confident in your skin as you sail to your grand purpose. One your most significant purposes should be to pour into others and to give back because you know that within you lies a person that went through the school of hard knocks and came out resilient on the other side. Coming into a new world, to learn a different language, to get accustomed to a new culture was part of my destiny and it will be yours too. Now it's time to reclaim your crown. Are you prepared to wear it loudly and proudly? Lead like the powerful female immigrant queen that you are and were always meant to be!

Shirley Baez

Hello, I am **Shirley Baez**, I am passionate about helping people reach their full potential and achieve their goals. Whether you are looking to start a business, better your career, or make a change in your life, I am here to help. Through my personalized approach, I provide a safe and supportive space for you to explore your true purpose and develop the knowledge and confidence to strengthen your skills and reach your goals. I specialize in life, career, and business coaching and am committed to helping you live an inspired and empowered life.

Shirley can be reach at:

ShrleyBaez.com & PowerfulFemaleImmigrants.com

ROCKY ROAD

Christie Perez, Puerto Rico

Life doesn't always turn out the way You expect and hope but despite its twists and turns and Rocky Roads You can always find the Sweet Spots that will bring You Joy, Happiness, and Fulfillment.

I was feeling frightened, sad, and lonely as I boarded an enormous, long silver jet liner plane alongside my big brother. It was just the two of us and I was saying goodbye to the island I was born in and everything I ever knew. We were getting ready to start our new life in America. I was only 12 yrs. old at the time My mother was sending us off to America where she would later reunite with us. Rocky Road.

I was born in a very small island in the northeast Caribbean Sea. Puerto Rico was my first home. My mother is Puerto Rican, and my father was a Cuban immigrant who's family had fled Fidel's Castros ruling during the 60's. My parents didn't last long despite their professing love for one another. My father left my Mother, Brother and I when I was only 3 for another woman whom he eventually started another family with. Both my Parents remarried shortly after they divorced when I was just shy away from turning 5 yrs. old. Within a span of a Yr. I was attending both my Parents wedding and being introduced to total strangers. Rocky Road.

My mother had married us into a blended family, and We became a total of 6 kids overnight. 3 Girls on my stepfather's side and 2 of us on my mother's side with a baby boy to be born into our blended family 2 yrs. later. It was a lot of changes happening all at once for a 5 yr. old to handle. Years passed and I was finally settling in to our New life with our blended family. Until one summer day our mother told us she had an announcement to make. Our Stepfather had lost his job and we were moving to America. His daughters would stay in P.R with their mother and the rest of us would be moving to America. At first, I felt excited, thrilled and happy to hear we were going to America it was like a dream come true. Then I felt the separation, abandonment, loneliness, and fear of what was to come. That day marked a pivotal point in my life and the beginning of my Rocky Road.

Life in America wasn't easy especially for our Stepfather who couldn't speak English and had trouble finding jobs. My parents were always working, and we barely saw them so my brothers and I took care of each other. School was an adjustment as we were foreign kids coming into a town where we were amongst very few Hispanics. Trying to fit in I started hanging out with the wrong crowd, skipping school, smoking, and sneaking out my bedroom window were just a few of my treacheries. I wanted to be accepted and liked so badly that my behavior kept leading me onto Rockier Roads. At the age of 14 I decided to get a job to help my mother. One day while I was at work a friend of mine invited me to go to her church. I only went because I liked a boy who went there. Little did I know that the church I was about to attend was more of a cult than a church.

It was a Pentecostal Church where every member was pressured to attend 7 days a week otherwise You were going to hell, and I got sucked into their teachings and methodologies for Years. My mother allowed me to go as she thought it would be good for me. I later began dating this boy and became very close to his family and spent all my time with them. He had the family I always longed for. I was looking for love in the wrong places. I became pregnant at the age of 16. Rocky Road.

What was I going to do? I had never felt more alone, lost and scared. The father of my child was not supportive, and I hid my pregnancy for 6 months until I could no longer hide it. I remember driving to the Pastors house to relinquish the secret I kept for so long that was breaking me. He told me I had to get married and had my mother sign the papers to give me permission to do so. I had no idea what I was doing nor how my life would unfold. Rocky Road. I married a guy whom I was in love with, but he wasn't. He only married me because he was told he had to. We had a very small wedding ceremony. After the wedding ceremony on the following Sunday, I walked into the Church with shame and embarrassment as the Church Members looked at me with disgust and pity as they could see I had gotten married because I was pregnant. There was no more hiding my belly. The secret I kept for so long had been exposed. I missed my Prom, and all the important activities and events teenagers should experience. Rocky Road. I was a Kid having a Kid. Despite my shortcomings I decided to go to a Community College to finish my high school diploma.

Shortly after I turned 17, I had my daughter. She was born on Labor Day September 6, 1999. The Delivery was harsh. I was 14 hrs. in labor with no doctor in site while my daughter was wrapped around her umbilical cord for a long period of time and had inhaled meconium. After 14 long arduous hours my Doctor finally showed up and had to deliver the news that he had to do an emergency c-section. I was terrified.

I delivered my daughter at 7:30pm on that Labor Day. I was happy and thrilled. This was finally over. Except it wasn't. As they delivered my Baby I couldn't hear a cry. The baby wasn't breathing. The Doctors and Nurses kept trying to help her breathe and all I could hear as I was lying in that operating room table was Come on Baby Cry, Come on Baby Cry over and over until I finally heard a very slight faint cry. And then the commotion began, they rushed her out of the room. She was later rushed via ambulance to a different hospital as the current hospital didn't have the necessary equipment to care for her. I couldn't name my baby, hold her or see her until I was released from the hospital 5 days later. Baby Perez as the Nurses called her was held in NICU for a month. She was a fighter and to this day still is. Words cannot describe the love and admiration I feel for her. I was so happy and looking forward to a bright happy future with our family.

During the interim process My husband at the time and I decided to buy a new home that we could settle our family in. Only to find out on the day of closing that my husband had gotten fired from work. Rocky Road. Despite that we somehow managed to close. My husband had decided to go into business for himself and started his own company. One day after getting home from work with my daughter I found a note posted on our door. We were being foreclosed. My husband had never once made the payments of our mortgage. He had used all the money he was making to pour into his business and entertain his clients.

This was another big moment of impact for me. If we didn't make the payments we were going to lose our house and be left on the streets. However, by the Grace of God we were able to get the Foreclosure stopped right before it went to Auction. I was able to breathe for that minute. We were still able to hold on to our American Dream.

Our marriage as a very young couple was very rocky. We were teenagers raising a baby, working, playing house, and trying to do things adults do except we didn't know what we were doing. We were just trying to survive and make things happen in this country.

Despite all of our shortcomings I decided to put myself through college at the age of 19 while working a full-time job, taking care of my daughter, husband and home. I wanted more for my daughter and for us. I didn't want to become a statistic even though I had already fallen into that category for most. I was trying to turn my life around and I was determined in pursuing the American Dream my mother had once sold us when we left Puerto Rico. Throughout the interim process of working a full-time job, going to school, and taking care of my daughter I found out my husband was cheating on me with a Church Member. Rocky Road.

I felt like my lungs had collapsed and my entire world was being ripped out from right in front of me. I couldn't breathe, eat, sleep, or function but I needed to. I had a little girl that depended on me. I tried everything I knew to keep us together but there was no way around this for my husband. He filed for divorce.

Once again, I came home one late afternoon and was surprised by a second foreclosure notice slapped on my door but to my surprise it wasn't the second. It was a third foreclosure notice. He never made the arranged payments the second time around and now this was our third and final foreclosure notice. Rocky Road. As if it wasn't enough with getting the divorce papers served, I was also now being served with a third foreclosure notice.

My knees where weak and I almost fell to the ground with my daughter standing right beside me. I didn't know what to do. My husband had filed for divorce, left the house, and left my 5 year old daughter and I all alone to fence for ourselves. I wanted to give up. I didn't see a way out. What was I going to do?

And to make things worse I had to attend the same church my husband and I were going to and see him there with his new girlfriend. I was told by the Pastor that if I stopped going to that specific church that I would be cursed by God. I was already feeling cursed, but I kept going. After many sleepless, anxious, depressing nights filled with fear, loneliness, and agony I decided to move forward and fight to keep the house for my daughter and me. If I wanted to keep the house, I was told I needed to get divorced quickly and had to refinance it under my own name. Our marriage lasted 5 yrs. and at the age of 23 I was already getting divorced. I kept the house but now was faced with a payment of $1,200 and a 12% interest.

How was I going to make that payment, pay the necessities and put food on the table when I was only making $9 dollars and hour. Rocky Road. By the way, this is my favorite ice cream. I ate lots of it during this very long rocky road and learned that despite the rocky roads in life You will always be met by some sweet spots.

I was able to get two roommates who were able to help me make the mortgage payment and gave my daughter a happy unorthodox family. This wasn't the traditional family I envisioned giving my daughter however we created a happy environment for all of us and most importantly for her. Right after my divorce and everything I went through in trying to keep the house I decided to get my Real Estate License. I knew that someday, somehow I would get into real estate and create wealth through it.

I kept working and going to school. I had so many odd jobs during the interim process from selling magazine subscriptions, to hauling vacuum cleaning machines across town in my station wagon and giving 3-hour presentations in strangers homes to selling eye surgeries. It took me 8 long yrs. to graduate college and obtain my bachelor's degree. Everyone thought I was going to school to become a Doctor because of how long it took me to graduate. I then went on to obtain my master's degree. This helped me get a good paying job and I started climbing the Corporate Ladder. Then 2015 came along and after having a good and stable paying job for several yrs. I got laid off. Rocky Road. Here we go again. However, this time was different. I was wiser, educated and more resilient than ever. I knew where I came from and how long it took me to get there. But most importantly I knew my why and what I was fighting for. It was my turning point. I decided to get into Real Estate Full Time. I learned the ropes, worked with Buyers and Sellers and eventually began working with investors.

I became so passionate about real estate and learned everything I could to never have to go back to Corporate America. I brought a second home for my daughter and I and rented the home I was foreclosed on 3 times which I later sold and nearly tripled my money.

Today I am a Full Time Real Estate Investor happily engaged to a wonderful man who respects loves and values me. And my daughter and I have become the best of friends.

My Journey to America wasn't an easy one but after so many Rocky Roads I came to understand that I didn't need easy I needed possible. And in this Beautiful Country I now call home I came to see all the possibilities and opportunities life must give if You open yourself and allow them to come in.

Through my Rocky Road journey, I also learned that Life is a choice, and that every day You must decide to either keep going or give up. I decided to keep going and never give up despite the Rocky Roads ahead. Its through these Rocky Roads that You grow and get to experience some of the sweetest thing's life has in store for You. Through my Rocky Road I received my most precious gift my daughter. And through this Rocky Road, I found myself. And finding Yourself and knowing Who You are is one of the most rewarding and self-satisfying treasures life can give You that no money can buy. I encourage You to define Your Rocky Roads because it's during these that You will find and meet Yourself.

Christie Perez

Born and raised in the small tropical island of Puerto Rico Christie Perez immigrated to Florida with her family at the very early age of 12 in search of the American Dream. Christie Perez graduated from the University of Central Florida with a Bachelor in Business Marketing and a Masters in Project Management. Despite her degrees and Corporate America Job, she pursued a different career path as a Real Estate Entrepreneur.

Her passion for Real Estate and her love and desire to help people achieve their American Dream of Home-Ownership led her to become a Real Estate Agent in 2004 and shortly thereafter a Real Estate Investor.

Her Proudest accomplishment was becoming a mother to her wonderful daughter. She became a single mother at a very early age and raising her on her own was both challenging and rewarding, but an experience she wouldn't trade for anything. This was the determination and drive that led her to pursue and achieve her dreams.

Her story is one of resilience, determination, and an unwavering commitment to living a life guided by love, respect, and integrity which is at the core of everything she does. Some valuable lessons she's learned throughout her journey have always been to follow Your intuition, learn to love Yourself and never give up despite life's circumstances.

One of her profound messages is that Self-love is the foundation upon which we build our relationships with others, and it's crucial to invest in ourselves so we can give more to those around us. Her mission is to Empower and encourage Women and individuals from all walks of life to always follow their passion, explore new things, better themselves, never give up, and most importantly never stop seeking knowledge.

Each chapter of her life has taught her many valuable lessons that allowed her to grow and as she continues on her journey, she is excited to see what new adventures await and how she can use her experiences to inspire others along the way.

Christie can be reach at:

ChristiePerez.com & *PowerfulFemaleImmigrants.com*

HOPE, HOLD ON, PAIN ENDS

Bibi Ofiri, Nigeria

My name is Blessing Bibi Ofiri. I was born in Nigeria to a family of seven. My Dad and mum are missionaries who moved to the US in 1996 to preach the gospel of Christ. They tried bringing us to the US before we turned 21 years old but was not possible. I would say I had a good childhood. My dad was able to provide for us the basis and ensured we didn't lack anything, but things took a turn after his death.

I went to College in Nigeria where I got my first bachelor's in project management technology from Lagos State University, Lagos-Nigeria. We experienced several strikes in our schools and the effect was that we spent longer time than necessary to graduate. Eight years in college instead of five years, due to the constant strike, I decided to pick up a part-time job in order to make money. I started modeling and assisting event management companies. I was able to make some money during that time until I lost my dad in 2009. That took a turn in my life because he was the breadwinner and despite the fact I was working, I still needed support. After his death, I decided to start up a cleaning company out of my passion for loving a clean environment. Also, I had always known I would be an entrepreneur, and that made it easier for me to take the bold step of starting up a business while still in school. I would confess that it was not a bed of roses. It was challenging, I had no money, no experience, no office, no employee, no car, and absolutely nothing. I remember that I would work many miles each day to visit new prospects, marketing and selling my services. I received a lot of disappointments at the beginning but with resilience, hard work, and determination, I began to see the light.

I started my first business in 2010 and gradually grew my cleaning business where I was able to employ over 100+ contract workers and about 10 permanent staff. This was possible because I was able to increase my growth after I participated in a business competition (Youwin) where I won a 10-Million Naira grant from the federal government of Nigeria in 2011. Life was good and promising.

I got married to my husband in 2012 after I won the grant and had my first child in 2014. The cleaning business was becoming more stressful and competitive, so I decided to expand the business to a property management company. We were managing estates, shopping malls, schools, churches, banks, etc. And the business boomed.

I got pregnant with my second baby and decided to move to the US to deliver my baby. My Previous experience with my first child was not a pleasant one and almost cost me my life and that was why I decided to get better health care in the US for my second pregnancy. I came to the US in 2018 to deliver and was supposed to leave 3weeks after her delivery but I didn't know God had other plans and that my life was going to take a 360° turn.

My dad died in 2009 and after a while, my mum was no longer able to keep up with the payments for the houses they had. They both had 3 single families and a church. She decided to do a short- sale for two of the houses before I arrived in the US. I later realized that she was on the verge of losing her primary house as well. She was afraid to tell us because she felt we would be disappointed. I was confused and scared because I had no idea how real estate worked in the US at that time and how to manage the situation.

I arrived in the US two months before my delivery and did not know my life was going to change. We received a note of foreclosure with the auction date and time. Shortly before my daughter's delivery, we heard a knock at our door, and behold it was the sheriff. He requested to see my mum and handed the notice to evict within one month. We both burst into tears. We were helpless, it was short notice, and I was pregnant.

Two weeks later the sheriff's visit, my baby was born. During my delivery, I started losing my breath and was given oxygen to help me breathe. I gave birth to my daughter nine hours after I arrived at the hospital. The nurses quickly did skin-to-skin with my baby and me and immediately took her to the ICU. I thought they took her to clean her up or something but became worried after I did not see her for a while. They took me to my room to rest but I couldn't because I wanted to know why my baby was not with me. The nurses told me that the doctor would visit me in my room shortly. After five hours, the doctor came in and told me that my baby had respiratory problems, and she had a 50/50 percent chance of survival. She also informed me that they will be transferring her to another hospital in Orange County California. I was in so much pain after I found out that my baby had a 50% chance of survival. At that point, I told the doctor that I was going to move with my baby, but the doctor requested that I stayed until the next day. To cut a long story short, I went to the hospital the next day and found my baby with different tubes in her system. I cried so much that the nurses had to console me and requested that I go home to rest.

I went back home and was shuttling between going every day to the hospital and parking our belongings from the house because we had only two weeks to leave. It was such a scary time because my baby was in a bad situation, we were about to lose our house and I was running out of money because I paid a lot of money for the delivery of my baby, and finally, we had nowhere to go on such short notice. I knew no one, and my mum was in a bad state because she couldn't comprehend the reality of losing her husband, houses, and the home in which she spent the last days with her beloved husband.

We decided to move our belongings to the church. We moved to the church and converted my mum's office into a room. We had no bathrooms but only toilets. We went to Home Depot and got a big bowl to use as a bathroom in the meantime. The office was very cold because it was not properly insulated to prevent cold. In all this misery, I was still shuttling between the hospital and our new home (the church). With the little funds we had, someone referred a contractor to us. I was able to bring back my daughter after a month and had nurses coming to visit. We were able to complete the construction within 3weeks before the arrival of my daughter. I thought the worst had happened until we got a visit from the city. I started to ask myself that when will all these trials come to an end? It seems like there was no end to our misery. The department of building and safety told us that someone informed them that there was an illegal structure and that they will have to come in to check. I confirmed the date, and they came only to inform us that the church was originally a warehouse and not a church. My parents did not do their due diligence before they bought the property eighteen years ago and suddenly, the city just got informed.

Again, I felt the whole world crumbling around me and at this point, I was confused. This was the last building standing for us and we did not have the money to bring it to code. We were given forty-five days to compile or demolish the property. We decided to engage an architect to figure out the best way forward.

So, I decided to look for any menial job to do because we needed to raise money for the architect to commence the drawing and money to take care of ourselves. My mum was in a bad condition with her health (Her blood pressure was extremely high), and my daughter was in no condition to leave the country, therefore, leaving the country was not an option. At this point, I was between the devil and the deep blue sea and in a completely confused state. My business partner in Nigeria was not also helping matters. He kept complaining that he was always approving of money to be transferred to me while he was doing all the work. I felt he was selfish and not compassionate. Unknowing me, he had other plans. I decided to pick up a security job, a cleaning job, and a restaurant job. We had a lot of bills to pay, including the church's mortgage. After my dad's death, the church lost a lot of members and was left with only nine consistent members. They were not capable of coming up with their mortgage most times, so I had to support that as well. So, I was doing all those jobs to pay bills and for us to feed. It was a very difficult time I must confess. Before I knew it my six months visa expired, and I had no choice but to stay and keep going. I called my business partner and told him I would not be able to come back at this time but that I would support the business as soon as I figured things out in the US. I was shocked at his response. He told me that it won't be possible for only him to keep going and I keep benefiting from the success of the business. It was a very ugly situation I found myself in because I was also having some major issues with my husband that cost us to separate. This was a period I would not have wished for my enemy.

So, I decided to let go of the business that I spent so many years building in Nigeria. I was in no situation to fight this battle with my business partner, I had a lot on my plate. At that point, I had lost everything: my husband, our home, my business, etc.

The most difficult part for me was the thought that I was just doing well a while ago and lost it over six months. I can remember crying almost every night. Sometimes, I would go into the church auditorium to cry and pray that things would get better. At some point, we had to look for support from the government because I could no longer make it work. We were not sure of eating the food of our choice but only what was available. I had to look for a caregiving home to put my baby in so I could work because my mother was no longer in a good state of care for my baby and my first daughter. I kept going on with my security job morning and night and in between, I would work in the restaurant to assist in washing dishes, pots, and pans for hours. After eleven months of my newfound life, I started making a little extra and decided to go back to school. I applied to the University of Phoenix and got an admission to study Information Systems with a degree in Cyber security. I was attending my classes in my car as a security guard at a construction site. It was not a comfortable place to study but I had no choice. I had to work and school at the same time to pay my school fees. My Mum picked up a job and was able to support me in some areas. At some point, I had to defer my classes for two months because I could not keep up with the payment. Fortunately, I was able to wrap up my two years course with a payment plan with the school and came out with all A's.

Six months towards the end of my course, I lost two of my jobs and I could not understand how that was possible because I was very diligent at it. I did not know that God had other plans for me.

During my conversation with a friend, he told me he was going to pick up his W-2 from his formal employer. I requested to go along, with the hope that I could apply to that same company. Fortunately, I met the owner, and he told us his secretary resigned a few days ago. I saw that as an opportunity for me to request the job because I noticed he needed help. He quickly conducted an interview and asked how soon I could resume; I told him like "Yesterday" and he laughed and asked me to resume the next day and that he would send me the application documents to fill out. I resumed the next day and continued thereafter.

Eventually, towards the end of my course, I started losing interest in the IT course and was looking for other opportunities in real estate. I did not know about how real estate is done in the US, but I only knew how it was done in Nigeria. I also realized that my boss was making good money from his business, so I decided to discuss my business idea with him. He was reluctant for almost a year but during that time I decided to acquire knowledge. I went on YouTube, and training, and kept talking to brokers and agents. After eight months, I went back to inform him, and he reluctantly started.

We started in late 2020 and got our first Vacation rental in March 2021 and from that day, we kept closing on properties every other month. We were able to invest in SMF, Fix, and Flip, and finally into multifamily. We currently own 105 rental units and flipped about a dozen homes, 595 units as a limited investor, and about closing on 243 units as a lead sponsor in a syndication deal. I was also able to support my mum in purchasing six units.

What Makes Me A Powerful Immigrant
- The ability to keep going even when it seems impossible.
- The ability to rebuild from ground zero twice without giving up.
- Giving up was not an option.
- In everything, I know it is the grace of God that has led me thus far. I am sure I wouldn't have been able to do it alone.

What I Learned During That Time
- The path to my goal may not seem like the right way.
- I am the price, and I can rebuild wherever I find myself.
- Never give up. Keep pushing.
- Ask for help.
- Resilience, patience, and hard work
- To keep educating myself
- We can achieve anything that we set out to do.
- And above all the grace of God.

And finally, I would like to end with one of my favorite verses in the Bible:

"For I know the plans I have for you," declares the Lord, "plans to prosper you and not to harm you, plans to give you hope and a future." Jeremiah 29:11 NIV

Bibi Ofiri

Blessing Bibi Ofiri was born in Nigeria to a family of 7. She graduated from Lagos State University Lagos- Nigeria and obtained a bachelor's degree in project management technology and a master's in information systems with a degree in Cyber- Security from the University of Phoenix.

As a young entrepreneur, she started her cleaning business in 2010 and gradually transitioned to a property management company in 2013.

She is currently the COO at Blue Ocean Equity LLC with 4+ years as an Active Investor across asset classes (Land/SFR/Commercial/Multifamily). She specializes in asset management, technical analysis, and underwriting.

She is a hard-working, and highly motivated entrepreneur who will stop at nothing in getting things done. She is a follower of Christ and believes in God's love for everyone.

She is a mother of two beautiful girls. Her hobbies are listening to the news and singing.

Bibi can be reach at:

instagram.com/bibi_ofiri & *PowerfulFemaleImmigrants.com*

ZEN-BUILD: HOW TO CREATE A GOOD ENERGY HOME

Anastasia Makarska, Ukraine

Welcome, my dear bad-a**, awesome woman! I am thrilled that you have picked up this book. Perhaps you are someone who grew up feeling timid or has overcome past abuse. Maybe you are a strong woman who feels empowered when competing in a male-dominated profession. Or, like me, you may be a combination of both, depending on the different phases of your life. Regardless of who you are or what you've been through, I want you to know that this book is for you. It is my hope that the words within these pages will empower and inspire you to be the best version of yourself, no matter what challenges you may face along the way.

As a child growing up in Ukraine, which was then part of the former Soviet Union, I was enamored with the works of Tolstoy and Dostoyevsky, dreaming of a better life. I have also a deep appreciation for the culture of Russia: I love both Ukraine and Russia. I cannot live without Ukrainian borsht and Russian Matryoshka dolls, but most importantly, I cannot live without the warmth and sense of community among those people. The literature, poems, and fine arts of the former Soviet Union depict the soul, spirituality, and love in a unique and beautiful way. I grew up believing that despite being separate countries now, all former Soviet Union nations are brothers and sisters. If you ever find yourself in a Russian-speaking home, I assure you that you will be instantly charmed by the warm and loving people, regardless of their nationality. Embrace the opportunity to explore the beauty of Russia, Ukraine, Belarus, Kazakhstan, and over 190 other Russian-speaking nations located closely geographically that were once united politically but have their own unique traditions, cuisine, apparel, and holidays. I have always felt that the union of all these nations is a testament to how different cultures can coexist and live together in kindness and peace.

As an immigrant to the United States, I brought with me the tender sensibilities of my Eastern European upbringing. Drawing from my background in quantum physics and medicine (I formerly worked as a neurophysiologist), I founded Zen-build.com, a construction company with a mission to infuse more love into people's homes through building and remodeling while incorporating the best energy techniques of Eastern and Western cultures. The term "Zen" holds a profound significance, highlighting the importance of meditation, mindfulness, and intuition to attain inner peace. At Zen-build.com, we don't adhere to any particular religion, instead, we integrate the most valuable insights from various fields of science, technology, and spirituality to create our unique approach to living spaces, which we refer to as "Zen", or "Zen-build.com". It includes what my company can help you with, as well as what you can create and incorporate in your home yourself.

Throughout history, people have observed their environment and the nature around them and studied the cause-and-effect of seemingly coincidental circumstances that affect their lives. At Zen-build.com, we take inspiration from these ancient studies and incorporate them into our designs to create homes with good energy, fluency, and high vibrancy. By aligning with the natural world and promoting positive energy flow, our homes can improve your health, vitality, and even the colors of your everyday life. One of our clients who recently hired us to remodel her kitchen wrote, "I love to cook in my new Zen space! I easily lost weight, my health improved, and I feel fantastic!" Another customer loved the fact that her new home has so much natural light now that she feels much happier with her life! We are thrilled to share that our mission at Zen-build.com is to impact one million people with similar life-changing results.

The heartfelt reason behind my mission to create more loving homes stems from my experience when I first arrived in the United States. Picture this - you arrive to a foreign country with just $50 in your pocket, a three-year-old child, no English language skills, no credit history, no car, no driver's license, no computer, no phone, and no family or friends to rely on. This was my reality. It was a cold and snowy February, and in Ukraine, $50 could sustain us for a month, but in New Jersey, it was only enough to afford a motel for one night. I remember vividly walking with my young child in the snow, hoping to buy some bread at a grocery store 5 miles away with the few pennies we had. As we arrived, we discovered that there was no food available for the little money we had, and we started walking back to our "homeless hub." That's when a miracle happened. A kind limo driver pulled over and gifted me with the $400 I needed to stay in the United States just 5 minutes before my flight back to Ukraine. This experience helped me embrace the generosity of the American people and inspired me to create more loving homes for them.

Living through being homeless and struggling to survive in a foreign country stayed with me, and it inspired me to want to create homes that are loving and welcoming for others. I wanted to provide a space where people can feel safe and comfortable, where they can create memories with their loved ones and thrive. I believe that the environment we live in has a profound impact on our well-being and that by creating a space that promotes balance and harmony, we can live more fulfilling lives.

Let me now share with you my top five benefits of Zen Home.

What Does a Home with Good Energy Do for You?
1. Promotes Relaxation and Reduces Stress

By arranging furniture, decor, and other objects in a way that promotes relaxation and calm, we can reduce stress and anxiety. A cluttered and disorganized home can make us feel overwhelmed and stressed, while a well-organized and harmonious space can help us feel calm and centered.

For example, using soft colors, natural materials, and comfortable furniture can help create a soothing and relaxing living space. Adding plants and natural light can also promote a sense of calm and well-being. This can help reduce stress and promote better mental health for the whole family.

2. Improves Sleep Quality

Getting enough quality sleep is essential for good health and well-being. A Zen home can help promote better sleep by creating a peaceful and comfortable bedroom environment. This includes choosing a supportive mattress and bedding, arranging the bed in a way that promotes restful sleep, and minimizing distractions and clutter in the bedroom.

For example, it is recommended to place the bed in a position where you can see the door but are not directly in line with it. This helps create a sense of safety and security, which can promote better sleep. It is also recommended to minimize electronic devices in the bedroom and use blackout curtains or shades to minimize light pollution and promote restful sleep.

3. Enhances Relationships and Family Harmony

Zen home is not just about creating a beautiful and harmonious living space, but also about promoting positive relationships and family harmony. By using Zen home principles to create a welcoming and pleasant environment, we can help strengthen family bonds and promote positive interactions.

For example, using soft lighting, comfortable seating, and a round or oval dining table can help create a warm and inviting atmosphere for family meals. Adding family photos and sentimental items can also help promote a sense of connection and belonging. By creating a home that promotes positive relationships and family harmony, we can improve our overall well-being and happiness.

4. Boosts Productivity and Success

In addition to promoting good health and well-being, Zen home can also help boost productivity and success. By creating a living environment that promotes positive energy and balance, we can improve our focus, motivation, and creativity. This can help us achieve our goals and reach our full potential.

For example, using natural light, comfortable seating, and a clutter-free workspace can help promote focus and productivity. Adding plants or a water feature can also help promote creativity and inspiration. By creating a living environment that promotes productivity and success, we can improve our overall quality of life and achieve our goals more easily.

5. Promotes Good Health and Well-Being

Finally, living in a Zen home can help promote good health and well-being for the whole family. By creating a living space that is in harmony with the natural world, we can promote positive energy and balance in our lives, which can have a positive impact on our physical health as well.

For example, incorporating natural materials such as wood and stone can help promote a sense of grounding and balance. Using air-purifying plants can also help improve indoor air quality and promote better respiratory health. Additionally, avoiding the use of toxic chemicals and using natural cleaning products can help promote a healthier living environment.

Incorporating Zen home principles into your home can also help you identify areas of your home that may be impacting your health negatively. For example, if you are experiencing frequent headaches, the placement of your bed or workspace may be contributing to this issue. By making adjustments to your living space, you can help alleviate these symptoms and improve your overall health and well-being.

Living in good energy, and good vibes, a Zen home can have numerous benefits for the whole family, including improved relaxation and reduced stress, better sleep quality, enhanced relationships, and family harmony, boosted productivity and success, and improved physical health and well-being. By creating a living environment that is in harmony with the natural world and promotes positive energy and balance, we can improve our quality of life and achieve greater success and happiness.

If you think of *building* your own Zen house, consider these seven tips:

1. Set Your Intentions

The first step in building a Zen house is to set your intentions for the space. What do you want to achieve with this space? Do you want to promote relaxation and calm, boost productivity and success, or enhance family harmony? Understanding your goals and intentions for the space will help you make design decisions that are in alignment with these intentions.

2. Choose Your Location

When choosing a location for your Zen house, it's important to consider the surrounding environment. Look for a location that is in harmony with the natural world, with good energy and balance. Avoid locations with negative energy or that are surrounded by clutter or chaos.

3.   Consider Your Building Materials

Choosing the right building materials is essential for creating a Zen house. Natural materials such as wood, stone, and bamboo are ideal, as they help promote a sense of grounding and balance. Avoid synthetic materials or materials that are treated with chemicals, as they can have a negative impact on indoor air quality and overall well-being.

4.   Optimize the Layout

The layout of your Zen house is crucial for creating a harmonious living space. In Zen-build.com, it's recommended to have a flowing, open floor plan that allows for natural movement and promotes positive energy flow. Avoid narrow hallways or cramped spaces that can impede movement and promote stagnant energy.

5.   Choose Colors and Décor Wisely

Colors and décor can have a powerful impact on the energy and atmosphere of your Zen house. Choose for soft, natural colors such as earthy browns, greens, and blues, as they help promote a sense of calm and relaxation. Avoid bright or bold colors that can be overstimulating or create a sense of chaos.

6.   Incorporate Natural Light and Fresh Air

Natural light and fresh air are essential for promoting good health and well-being in a Zen house. Incorporate large windows and skylights to allow for ample natural light and consider adding air-purifying plants to help improve indoor air quality.

7. Pay Attention to Details

The details of your Zen house are important for creating a harmonious living space. Pay attention to the placement of furniture, artwork, and décor. Use rounded corners and avoid sharp edges, as they can create negative energy. Additionally, keep the space clean and free of clutter to promote positive energy flow. Don't forget about plants! Live plants are essential in your living space. You can even create a garden that complements the home's design and incorporates features like water, rocks, and plants to promote positive energy flow.

Building a Zen house takes careful planning and attention to detail, but the rewards of creating a harmonious living space can be immense. By incorporating these principles into your design and décor choices, you can create a space that promotes relaxation, productivity, and overall well-being. Zen-build.com can sure help you with that!

In addition to Zen-build.com company's focus on housing, we also build and operate small-setting assisted living homes that prioritize the comfort and well-being of our elderly loved ones. I am excited to share my upcoming book, "Assisted Living, a Home Sweet Home for Your Aging Parent," which highlights the importance of creating a loving and nurturing environment for our seniors. One of our residents just happily celebrated her 100th birthday together with our staff, which was a true delight! We have received so much positive feedback from our assisted living homes, and it's truly humbling to see the impact our philosophy and approach has on the lives of our residents and their families. Our goal is to not only provide exceptional care, but to also create a warm and inviting atmosphere where residents can truly feel like home.

At the end of the day, my passion for building and creating beautiful spaces comes from a deep belief in the power of the human spirit. I truly believe that by creating spaces that promote peace, love, and positive energy, we can all live happier and more fulfilling lives.

As we create anything in this world, our top priority should be to foster peace. Love is the key to solving the world's problems, guiding us to identify what we do not want - like grief, loss, and wars - and empowering us to build the world we do want. When asked what new tradition I would like to see embraced, I suggested the practice of applauding at each plane landing. This simple gesture goes beyond thanking the pilot and crew for a safe flight; it also represents our support for countries that are often distanced from us by media and politics. Let us demonstrate our commitment to peace and love by clapping at plane landings and spreading kindness wherever we can.

In a peaceful world, everyone deserves to have a home that promotes well-being and success, and that's what we strive to achieve with every project we take on. It's been an incredible journey, and I'm so grateful for the opportunity to use my experience to make a positive impact on the lives of others.

Anastasia Makarska

Anastasia is an extraordinary individual who has made remarkable contributions across various fields. Hailing from Ukraine, she migrated to the United States to pursue higher education, where she embarked on a PhD in Physics program at the prestigious Georgia Institute of Technology in Atlanta, Georgia. Later, she graduated from Eastern Virginia Medical School in Norfolk, Virginia, where she gained extensive experience in surgery and intraoperative neurophysiology over a decade.

In addition to her impressive academic and professional background, Anastasia has established two highly successful companies - Zen-Build.com, a construction firm, and Pinnacle Home Realty, a real estate brokerage and property management firm licensed in multiple states. She also co-founded Eight Three Capital (83cap. com), a real estate investment company that empowers investors to achieve their goals. Through these ventures, Anastasia has made significant contributions to the fields of construction, property management, and real estate investment.

Anastasia is a passionate advocate for giving back to the community and is a sustainable patron of the Carnegie Library of Pittsburgh, providing valuable educational resources to the public. She is a prolific author with several upcoming books that will delve into topics such as assisted living for aging parents and commercial real estate underwriting.

When she is not pursuing her professional pursuits, Anastasia loves engaging in creative hobbies such as playing the piano, writing songs, and painting on canvas. Her multifaceted achievements reflect her unwavering dedication to excellence and her great commitment to creating a positive impact in various areas of society. Anastasia's exceptional accomplishments and contributions serve as an inspiration to others seeking to make a difference.

Anastasia can be reach at:

linktr.ee/Anastasia.Makarska & *PowerfulFemaleImmigrants.com*

HOW TO LIVE A MIRACULOUS LIFE WORTH WRITING ABOUT?

Natalia S. Pazos, Argentina

I was born in Cordoba, Argentina and when I was 11 years old my parents decided to move to Miami, Florida. My family was persecuted due to my father's political involvement and my parents were almost killed several times during the course of operation of their businesses. I remember we had to go around the block every day before entering our home to observe with a closer look if anyone was there waiting for us. I remember exactly the last time I witnessed an armed robbery. My mom stood in front of the door that separated my sister and I, from the perpetrators. She did not let them in. When she opened the door she was covered in blood, they had thrown her on the floor, beat her up and cut open her head. Shortly after we migrated to the United States. This was not easy for an 11 year-old to understand at the time, and I can see clearly now how this decision my parents made forever altered the course of my life.

We underwent a 10-year immigration process to finally become US residents. During this time, both my grandparents passed away, and my parents were not able to be there with them or say their goodbyes. It was very difficult to watch my parents go through that pain. I witnessed them experience a sense of "helplessness", that there was nothing they could do to change that situation. However, no matter the hardship my parents underwent, they have always demonstrated how to overcome and have the resilience necessary to get back on their feet.

We did not speak English at the time we moved to the US, yet my parents became successful business owners and were able to build an empire, part of which I supported to build. As the oldest of two siblings, I became the person they consulted when they needed support to get things done. I started translating letters, speaking with vendors, making calls, making payments and collecting payments on their behalf at the age of 11. I later started hiring and training new personnel, managed their stores while I was in College. And I have managed their real estate investments as an adult. From a very young age, the more responsibility I took and the more matters I handled for them, the more I was rewarded and loved. And thus, it became second nature to me to "take responsibilities" and "fix problems" for others. In this case, for my parents. I spoke on their behalf, advocated for their rights and the rights of our family-owned businesses.

Eventually, I became the ultimate "fixer" - a lawyer. One who is compensated for handling matters for other people. I had become an attorney because I had witness my parents go through so many, what I considered at the time, "painful and unfair situations." And I wanted "justice," I wanted to help others to "make things right."

I graduated from the University of Miami top of my class, and completed my Juris Doctor at FIU College of Law. I was a judicial intern in the Eleventh Judicial Circuit of Florida, worked at the Florida Supreme Court and later opened my own practice. Although on paper this might have looked good and made my parents very proud, I found myself unfulfilled, highly stressed, and unhealthy. I had developed a chronic back pain and was 70-pounds overweight.

So how did I get from… being unfulfilled, 70-pounds overweight, with chronic back pain, $60,000 in credit card debt, to … quadrupling my income, paying off all my credit card debt, while doing something I love and losing 70 pounds in ONE YEAR?

The answer is simple: I took ownership of my life; refrained from blaming; and started living a Miraculous Life.

A friend and mentor once said to me: "Don't write about the life you are living. Live a life worth writing about." And I have adopted this philosophy of life. The question I ask myself constantly is:

How Do I Live A Miraculous Life Worth Writing About?

With time, I have discovered that in order to live a miraculous life worth writing about, I get to: (1) be in relationship with God; (2) live on purpose; (3) surround myself with extraordinary people; and (4) live life as if someone is always learning from me, because they are!

Live In Relationship With God

The more time I have devoted to my connection with the Divine, the more successful I have become. Success has been a direct result of my devotion and connection to Spirit.

I devote time to God every day. My relationship with Him is the most important relationship in my life. Just like I spend time in my life to cook every day to feed and nourish my body, I get to spend time with God every day to feed and nourish my soul. In doing so, my trust in Him grows and my relationship with Him strengthens. Nourishing and building a relationship with God takes time and devotion. Just like with every relationship in our lives.

Being in constant conversation with God has allowed me to build my relationship with Him. I like to begin my day by asking God to guide me and allow me to be in service to people, to assist them and walk them home. I ask the following questions when I begin my day, before a showing or a meeting: "What would You have me do? Where would You have me go? What would You have me say, and to whom?" *Lesson 71, from A Course in Miracles*. He answers in the most miraculous ways and never ceases to amaze me.

My relationship with God has not always been like this. I grew up Catholic, attended Catholic school, went to church every Sunday, and everything that came along with it. After moving to the United States, this started changing. I started getting older and questioning whether everything I was repeating by memory I really meant, and whether everything I was doing was in alignment with what I believed to be true. I realized I had a "textbook-like relationship" with Jesus. I had learned in school what to say, what to do, how and when to communicate with God. And I wasn't really feeling it. I had a superficial and disconnected relationship with Him.

This is when I started my spiritual journey. It was during a difficult time in my life, when many abrupt changes were taking place. My family was losing the empires they had built throughout the years in the United States, my parents were going through a challenging time in their marriage, and I wasn't sure if I wanted to practice law anymore. I had spent thousands of dollars in education, countless of hours studying and preparing for the Bar exam and I found myself questioning everything. I questioned my spiritual beliefs, my career decisions, and kept asking myself: "what is my purpose in life?" And not knowing the answer to this question inspired me to seek. And those who seek shall find. And I did. I found God. And then God led me back into Real Estate.

I believe we are all walking each other Home. I have realized, with the support of my mentors, that walking my clients Home, goes far beyond "selling a house" or "finding clients a great multi-family Real Estate investment." It begins with a process of assisting them in realizing what it is they desire, what it is they are seeking and supporting them every step of the way. On this journey, I discovered my purpose is to guide others Home. As they fulfill their mission, I'll fulfill mine.

Live On Purpose With Direction

On this path of transformation, growth and self-development, I found that to live a miraculous life I get to live on purpose. I found the answers on how to live on purpose were not out there, but within. I found that purpose is not something we do, but rather something we are. I found that purpose is not about "what" we do, but "who" we serve and "how" we serve them. I found that living on purpose is being an extension of love to everyone I encounter in everything I do. I found that living on purpose is making an impact in the lives of others. I found that living on purpose is when I align my thoughts with those of God. Living on purpose is contributing to the shift from any thought that hardens the heart, denies love and deflects miracles, to those that soften the heart and attracts them. When someone lives on purpose and makes an impact, they are contributing to the natural occurrence of miracles.

I live on purpose when I have a vision that far exceeds my own personal achievements. I am a strong believer that to achieve great things in life, including living on purpose, we get to declare BIG goals for ourselves. I have recently heard repeatedly that "success follows speed." However, I have also come to learn that without clarity and structure, there is no progress. Without direction we cannot execute decisions quickly that are in alignment with our vision. If we act quickly without direction is like running around in circles with our heads cut off. We cannot be certain where we are in relation to where we want to be, unless we know clearly where we are headed and how we desire to get there.

Structure and consistency builds confidence to act. The formula to successfully live on purpose is to: have a clear vision + declare BIG goals + execute decisions quickly in alignment with the vision + take massive action immediately in alignment with the vision. This is taking ownership of your life!

And this is precisely what I did when I decided to start living a healthy life. I was clear I wanted to release 70 pounds. I had a clear vision and hired a professional nutritionist to help me achieve that goal. In one year I made it happen by having a vision, declaring goals, and taking massive action in alignment with the vision. And my health journey certainly does not stop there.

On December 31, 2022, I declared and committed to participate on my first ½ marathon in Switzerland. I committed to participate on two Spartan races with a team to prepare for the ½ marathon. The moment I committed to do this with a team, it far exceeded my own personal goals. This vision strengthen the team and deepened relationships with team members, by holding each other accountable and creating community. Once I had a clear vision, I made the decision to commit to the races immediately. I purchased the tickets and started taking massive action by training every other day. As I inspire other team members and hold them accountable, I get inspired in return. The power of vision and team is truly magnificent. Being outwardly focused supports the overall vision and my personal commitment simultaneously. As they win, I win. And as I take ownership of my life, I demonstrate and inspire others to do the same.

Live In Relationship With Extraordinary People

Proximity is power. I believe one of the most important factors to live a miraculous life is to surround ourselves with extraordinary people. I like to surround myself with people that inspire me, encourage me, challenge me and support my BIG goals. I am surrounded by positive thinkers, dreamers and visionaries, and driven and passionate leaders. I have mentors that I admire who inspire me to create a miraculous life worth writing about. I believe there is always someone two steps ahead that can support me, the same way, there is someone standing where I was two steps ago that I can guide.

I have noticed one of the qualities these way-showers, truth-tellers, determined, ambitious, and brilliant thinkers have in common is an unwavering commitment to support and inspire others. They are what Plato refers to as "the torch-bearers of humanity", those who "lead and lift the race out of the darkness and towards the light." And that is precisely what I intent to be every day in the lives of others as I ask God How may I serve? And I let Him show me the way.

Motivational speaker, Jim Rohn, said: "we are the average of the five people we spend the most time with." And I don't take this lightly. I love to co-create life with extraordinary people. My success is certainly the added efforts of my closest circle. My family and friends that inspire and encourage me to be my best. My coaches and mentors, without their support and commitment to serve and lead by example, I would not be where I am today. And most importantly my success and growth is a direct result of the intimate relationships in my life. My intimate relationships are my greatest teachers.

Live Life As If Someone Is Always Learning

Living a miraculous life is remembering that we are always teaching and someone is always learning from us. The *Course in Miracles* explains, to teach is to demonstrate and from this demonstration others learn, and so do we. It further emphasizes that to teach is to learn. Teaching and learning happen simultaneously. It further describes that all of us are students and all of us are teachers. Every moment we are teaching, because every moment we are demonstrating. And every moment we are a student, because in every moment we are being presented with circumstances in which we can learn.

I was taking a class with Marianne Williamson, a renowned spiritual teacher, author of *A Return to Love*, and teacher of *A Course in Miracles*. And I had the opportunity to speak with her and asked her: "When is a student of A Course in Miracles ready to teach? And how does the Course describe the student/teacher? And she responded: "What makes me a teacher of God is not that I give lectures on the Course in Miracles. What makes me a teacher of God is any moment I get this right. When I practice what I preach, I am a teacher of God, no different than you…. **No one can determine for you the level on which you decide to play life.**"

This reminds me every day IT IS UP TO ME TO CHOOSE the level at which I decide play life.

This is taking ownership.

This is knowing I am the creator of my life.

This is knowing I am the sculptor of my body.

This is knowing I am the creator of my wealth.

Although I enjoyed studying law, when I graduated, I knew there was something else for me. And thus, I began my own path of self-discovery and healing. So I did what I do best, I studied, read, researched, analyzed, and learned. I took every training possible, hired coaches and mentors, traveled the world, attended endless seminars, workshops and ceremonies. You name it, I have done it! The more I learned, the more I grew, the more I healed, the more I wanted to dive inward even further. However, it was not in the learning, but the unlearning. Marianne Williamson describes it beautifully in *A Return to Love*:

"When Michelangelo was asked how he created a piece of sculpture, he answered that the statute already existed in the marble. God Himself had created the Pieta… Michelangelo's job, as he saw it, was to get rid of the excess marble that surrounded God's creation… Your job is to allow the Holy Spirit to remove the fearful thinking that surrounds your perfect self, just as excess marble surrounded Michelangelo's perfect statute."

In this self-discovery process I learned to take ownership of my life by placing my future in the hands of God. I learned to let go and let God. And this was certainly no easy task, especially for a

Capricorn, former lawyer, recovered perfectionist/type A personality, who thought I knew better. I learned that to take ownership of my life requires TRUST. Choosing to take ownership of my life is a life long journey. One that I have chosen to walk. The good news is that the more I practice to take ownership and live a miraculous life, the easier it gets.

It has certainly not been an easy journey to get to where I am today, but it was well worth it. For me, taking ownership and living a miraculous life requires: developing a close relationship with God; living on purpose; surrounding myself with extraordinary people; and remembering that I am constantly teaching others by being and learning in all circumstances.

I am a Miracle Worker and I live a Miraculous Life. I am a full-time Real Estate investor and advisor who also offers consulting services to individuals and organizations ready to take ownership of their lives by creating extraordinary results in their Health and Wealth. I have created a signature program to guide people to take ownership of their miraculous lives. It brings me the most joy to support and guide others home, literally and figuratively speaking. I am committed to impact the lives of 1000 people in 2023 by supporting them to live a Miraculous Life.

Schedule a call or Join the movement to linktr.ee/nataliapazos

Natalia S. Pazos

Natalia S. Pazos is a Florida licensed attorney and a Miami Real Estate agent. She was born and raised in Cordoba, Argentina and moved to the United States in 1996. Natalia graduated from the University of Miami and completed her Juris Doctor degree at FIU College of Law. She worked at the Florida Supreme Court and opened her own practice in Miami in 2012. Natalia provided legal advice and represented clients in the areas of immigration, family law and real estate. She conducted real estate closings, prepared sale and purchase contracts and commercial lease agreements. She is a member of an attorney-owned and operated Real Estate Brokerage firm. She has negotiated and closed Real Estate transactions since 2005. In addition to her experience as an attorney and broker, she has owned and operated several rental properties in Miami, short-term and long-term. Her company also manages her client's Real Estate portfolios. Natalia's interest in Multi-Family Commercial Real Estate began when she joined Legends Equity Group.

Natalia's purpose is to guide people home and she does that literally and figuratively speaking. She guides clients home when they are purchasing or investing in Real Estate, and guides by demonstrating. She is, as *A Course in Miracles* describes, a student of the Course and a teacher of God, one who has answered the Call and has made a deliberate choice in which she does not see her interest as apart of someone else's. She is a mentor committed to making an impact in the lives of 1,000 people in 2023.

Natalia is a philanthropist and loves giving back to the community. She does so by impacting children's lives by tutoring, mentoring and teaching adolescents practical skills to create financial freedom and achieve generational wealth. Educating and guiding children is one of her ministries. It brings her the most joy to serve, inspire kids to dream big, and empower them with tools not currently learned in school. She was the Director of a non-profit organization, where she developed and launched a Mindfulness Program at Liberty City Elementary School. This program incorporated a mindful approach to education that was later implemented at other schools and youth centers in the district. She is currently developing new programs and is looking forward in using Multi-Family Real Estate as a conduit to make this dream a reality. She looks forward to being a catalyst for change and making a difference in the education system and children's lives.

Natalia can be reach at:

nataliapazos.com & *PowerfulFemaleImmigrants.com*

SERVE HUMANITY WITH PURE INTENTION, CLEAR VISION AND PROFOUND ACTION

Rosalind Panda, India

Editor's Note: Story told in first person and third person.

Have you wondered how meaningful your life could be when you live it with purpose to inspire, empower and impact others through what you do in your day-to-day life?

Her journey started when she was born in the city named Bhubaneswar, Odisha, India. She had two more sisters. Her parents are native to Odisha, India. Her father had served the Government as a soil conservation officer for 35 years of his life. Her mother was a housewife and extremely hard-working woman. Rosalind is truly inspired by her parents. In the initial period of her life, her family was financially sound, and a family based on love, affection and strong values. Despite every adversity her parents always made sure they built a solid foundation for their daughters. As her father oversaw government projects focused on rural development and soil conservation, the whole family had to move around from one city to another every few years

Luckily, the first school she started studying in was a private school based on Integral Education. Rosalind is truly content and proud of her 8 years of experience there at that school. Since her childhood she has been a quick learner, extremely smart and confident. Her father has always encouraged her to become the best version of herself. Starting from her elementary education, high school, college she has been a bright student and a strong personality. She was always recognized as the best scholar at school for years, forward thinker, outgoing. She shares her fun memories while she was in school. She would spend most of her time in studying the curriculum, history, literature, moral books, science, Math, social study books. In addition, she would focus on playing outdoor sports, she was extremely athletic and active all the time. Outside of her school time she would utilize her precious time creating art works, practicing classical music, composing songs and poems, playing the musical instrument called harmonium and singing. In the field of public speaking, she would research for hours on national issues. Her father, mother and teachers, friends were her greatest supporters and had been encouraging her throughout her life. She has used her childhood to fill her mind with boundless knowledge, curiosity to explore life in every aspect, understand how, why and why not certain things work the way they do

Her parents were early risers, and both made sure I am doing excellent in my school curriculum and using my energy to learn and acquire skills for life. When I look back into their contribution in my life I truly believe with their parental love and sacrifices they have built my life substantial and amazing.

I had great interest in learning new languages, vocabularies as well. My father would take me to the bookstore and buy me the books that became catalysts in my character building. In my school there were teachers who were amazed by my excellency in all areas and humble effort to excel and making everyone proud.

Growing up, life took an unknown twist and turn which I consider part of human journey of exploration. I was a forward thinker and visionary. I always see the big picture, the blessing in disguise whenever I experience adverse conditions in life. I had the courage to face everything with a brave heart and optimistic attitude.

I remember there are certain period of life the people in the society would criticize and find issues and be judgmental about my optimistic and courageous nature. On the other hand, due to my spiritual knowledge about life I would consider my life an individual's journey serving my purpose on earth and I do not get terrified by the thought of what people think. There are times when my parents would be shaken by society and the unseen and unknown. But I always had the courage to face the storm in life. I have built so much confidence in my mind, heart and my skills that I am always guided by my spirit.

My father had given me the advice that as human beings we don't need to focus on our appearances. We must go deeper to see the person who is inside that body, the spirit beneath the skin, the soul behind that face. The key is encouraging yourself every step of the way.

The Secret formula for winning life it is one of the most rewarding parts of running a road race in is that people lineup and cheer for us every step of the way wait as human being we need to learn how to do that for ourselves whether we cross the finish line or not we'll build our confidence faster than any medal or accomplishment ever could. Our relationship with ourselves is the foundation for everything in our lives how we talk to ourselves how we treat ourselves, how we love our own company sets the tone for everything we do.

My parents celebrated my birthday with all the love, affection and poured heavenly blessings on me to celebrate my existence. Since my childhood my dad has been the inspiration where he always made me feel or he told me like "you are unique and special as you deserve to be seen heard and celebrated" and I believe that every human being is unique in certain ways but some really are meant to bring the changes and some of us are capable of overcoming what we go through some people give up some people take it with complete determination and it doesn't matter to us. The external factors don't matter. We are rather propelled by the hurdles created to test us, to challenge us, to build the resilience in our attitude. catalyst Become scheduled list a wonderful catalyst in their life to move forward with even stronger good determination as human beings' confidence and creative design thinking in life are the keys. We can choose and we can change our environment we can change and it starts with the mind.

There are many obstacles came into my life and my parents' life. But despite out financial situation, they still gave me the education in a private school where we learned self-discipline, human value through meditation and serving the greater purpose through our actions and giving back to the society through wonderful contributions, through everyday practice, travel and adaptation to change. Going outside my comfort zone going outside the Box and going to sports meet, event at Rotary club, speaking events Knowing the world exploring the world going out of your zone, your surrounding where you are always going out of that and mixing with new people talking to new people new kids understanding their views their perspectives trying to build something together with them know that they are also they also exist and different cities and they have their uniqueness but I embraced everything that was coming my way.

For a short period of time some you might be coping with that situation but definitely it's not going to last until last long because it's called compromise you're trying to compromise with the situation rather than I'm really being honored with in it or having the sense of joy to be there right to be in that situation or in the environment and the surrounding so if you're when you become the leader of your own life you change your situation you take in your situation you take control of your life into your hand and no matter how other person are the person although external the society the parents the colleagues Theodore best friend or whoever it is like criticizing you My life journey and how my dad my parents their contribution helped me where I am so the book is powerful immigrant and

Rosalind Panda was born in the city of Bhubaneswar, Odisha on February 19, 1984, and grew up in Burla, Sambalpur till 1996 doing her elementary and middle school education. Her family moved to Bhadrak, Odisha afterwards and Rosalind was studying till 1999 there. Since her childhood, she has been an extremely creative individual in multiple areas and has been visiting different cities later in life to participate in various competitions, camps, sports meet and exhibitions. Rosalind is a global fine art artist, author, and public speaker. Among her career accomplishments, Ms. Panda is proud to have received numerous awards from her local chapter of Rotary International. she is a brown belt in mixed martial arts, Taekwondo. She is an expert at playing the musical instrument called Harmonium. She composes songs, gives the music and sings the songs. In addition, she has received the recognition in Indian classical music. Looking toward the future, she hopes to contribute her artwork to various charitable functions and auctions and to achieve greater recognition for her aptitude as an oil painter and a global fine art artist.

She has specialized in literature, mathematics, science and computer science during her college education.

Rosalind Panda

Rosalind enrolled in Foothill College in California, USA and was working as a part-time Mathematics instructor and software developer while pursuing her Information Technology career while in USA. She obtained her bachelor's degree and post graduate degree in Computer Application. Rosalind started her IT career when she was still pursuing her college education. Rosalind Panda has been in the Technology field more than 15 years of her life. She worked with numerous fortune 500 corporate clients such as, Google INC, United Health care, Belk.com, Citi Bank, Blue shield Health Care, UPMC (University of Pittsburgh Medical Center), PNC Bank, Sapphire Digital, Auto zone Inc, North Carolina Water Authority and many more as software lead and Architect. She has donated her art works in many corporate office locations and organizations like Google INC, Thermo fisher Scientific, University of Pittsburgh Medical Center.

She also is a board member of a non-profit organization that works to promote Art and Technology in the society. She is also featured in International Association of Women as an influencer and appeared as Top 10 CEOs of 2022 on NY Weekly and has received accolades from Marquis who is Who in America for her incredible contribution towards Art and technology growth in the community.

She has traveled the world to India, England, Mexico, Japan, China, USA. She studied in India and the USA, speaks multiple languages. She has a significant contribution in Information technology area as a technology evangelist as well.

Being an individual of purpose in life she influences people around her by making positive difference. She is passionate about helping others and utilizes her time to create art works, help clients and the community. She lives her dream by impacting people' s lives by adding value to them and by inspiring them to serve greater purpose on earth.

Rosalind can be reach at

linktr.ee/rosalindpanda & *PowerfulFemaleImmigrants.com*

WHAT IS A WOMAN'S MOST VALUABLE ASSET?

Kelli & Mari Ann Nguyen-Ha, Vietnam

Is it GRATEFULNESS?

Is it GENERATIONAL WEALTH? Is it PASSIVE INCOME?

Is it RESIDUAL INCOME?

Is it SELF-EMPOWERMENT? Is it FAMILY?

PLEASE ALLOW TO EXPLAIN MY OWN VERSION…

Introduction

My name is Kelli Nguyen-Ha. Together with my five sisters, Jennifer, Mari Ann, Monica, Melyssa, and Melynda, we are the creators of The FierceSix Mutifamily Equities. Of the six of us, Mariann and I are currently the active members of FierceSix MultiFamily Equities. Our company's mission is to empower one million women by 2033 to take control of their finances, and to help them create passive income through multifamily investing, which will in turn allow them to contribute to the world and become the best providers and givers. With our help, these women will be able to build generational wealth and live the lifestyles of their dreams. The name FierceSix represents the common character amongst the six girls in our family, and how we strive to continuously honor our late parents by working diligently and wisely every day. We relentlessly seek self-improvement and growth, both spiritually and financially, to become better human beings.

I have documented my journey as an immigrant in my first best Amazon's selling book titled, "Immigrant Millionaire: The Story of One Asian Woman Obsessed to Succeed in the Land of Opportunity." We consider ourselves FierceSix Sisters because it is the principles and life values that our late parents instilled in us that made us approach every aspect of our lives with a fearless, can-do attitude of self empowerment.

In my book, I talk about how I got into real estate back in 2008 as a complete beginner with a passion of becoming a millionaire, and in no time had achieved a multimillionaire status. As a family we wanted to achieve financial independence and freedom because it was the only way we would be able to support our loved ones. Our loved ones also include the less fortunate ones back in our native village in Vietnam, in our home state of Texas, and everywhere else in the world. As documented in my book, we are currently donating medicine, and rice for the elderly & the disabled in our ancestral village in Vietnam under our late parents' names. We know this was all possible because of the self empowerment we emulated from our parents.

The Brazilian football (soccer) player, Pelé once said, *"Success is no accident, it is hard work, perseverance, learning, studying, sacrifice and most of all, love of what you are doing or learning to do."*

Women's Most Valuable Asset- Self Empowerment

In this chapter, I'm going to talk about the most valuable asset you have, which is self empowerment. As FierceSix Sisters, we know that every woman has the innate capability to carry, provide, and empower all the men in our lives. Our grandmothers created our fathers, our mothers-in-law carried our husbands, our moms created our brothers, and we created our sons as individualized and powerful women.

But let me just reiterate that our most valuable asset as women is not the men in our lives, but ourselves. Every one of us must be self-reliant, self-sufficient, and self-dependent. We must be our own heroines and find strength within our own capabilities.

You see, every man has a woman in their life, whether it is their mom, their wife, their sister, or their daughter. And it's easy to lose ourselves in those roles, or to pour all of our time and energy into taking care of others. But the truth is you cannot pour from an empty cup. You must take care of yourself first in order to have the strength and energy to care for others.

Becoming Self Empowered

Believing in Yourself

So, how do you become self-empowered? It starts with believing in yourself. Believe that you are capable of achieving your dreams and goals. Believe that you have the power to overcome any obstacle that comes your way. Believe that you are worthy of love, respect, and success.

In 2008, when I made the decision to pursue a career in real estate, I lacked any prior experience or knowledge in this field. However, I had a strong belief that if others could achieve success in this industry, then I could too. Even if it means that my journey could take twice as long compared to others due to all my inherent barriers as an immigrant and as a 4'11" female playing in the male-dominated world of Business and Commercial Real Estate.

Another favorite quote goes, *"I'm not impressed by your looks, money, social status or job title. I'm impressed by the way you treat other human beings."*

Taking Action

Next, take action. Take steps towards your goals, no matter how small they may seem. Every step forward is progress, and progress leads to momentum. Momentum ultimately leads to success.

Sometimes, though, taking action can be scary. It means stepping out of our comfort zone, and facing your fears. Quite honestly that is where self-empowerment is born. When you are self-empowered, you have the confidence and courage to take action, even when it's difficult.

"F.E.A.R. has two meanings - Forget Everything And Run OR Face Everything And Rise. The Choice is yours." – *Zig Ziglar*

Taking massive action can be an incredibly empowering experience, particularly when it comes to boosting your confidence level. By diving in and taking action, you give yourself the opportunity to gain first-hand experience and knowledge, which can help to build your self-assurance and self-belief. There is simply no other way to gain this type of experience other than to take the leap and "just do it." While the prospect of taking massive action can be intimidating, particularly when facing a new or challenging situation, the rewards can be tremendous.

Here are four tips on how to become self-empowered:

Define your values and priorities. What is important to you in life? What are your goals and aspirations? When you know what you stand for and what you want to achieve, it becomes easier to make decisions and take action.

Surround yourself with positive influences. Spend time with people who support, encourage you, & who sincerely cares that you succeed. Seek out mentors and role models who have achieved what you aspire to achieve.

Take care of yourself. This means getting enough sleep, eating well, and exercising regularly. It also means taking care of your mental health, practicing self-care, managing stress, and seeking help when you need it.

Embrace your strengths and weaknesses. You are not perfect, and that's okay. Embrace your strengths and use them to your advantage. Acknowledge your weaknesses and work on improving them.

Self Empowerment Is A Journey

It's also important to remember that self-empowerment is not a destination, but a journey. It's something that you must work on every day. There will be ups and downs, successes and setbacks. For me to get to where I am now in life, I almost threw in the towel way too many times. I'd say, the low moments seemed to last forever, but looking back in retrospect I appreciate them as lessons. I can now reflect with a lot of real estate wisdom on the long days when I used to multitask as a room cleaner, breakfast attendant, laundry attendant, front desk clerk, auditor, and any other positions to redevelop a hotel. As recounted in my first book, I did what it took to turn the hotel's less than $300k annual revenue to over $1.2 million in less than three years.

Having Faith In Your Journey

Having faith in your journey is an essential aspect of self-empowerment for women. It means believing in yourself, trusting your intuition, and embracing the challenges and opportunities that come your way. Self-empowerment requires resilience, determination, and the ability to overcome obstacles. It involves taking risks, making mistakes, and learning from them.

By having faith in your journey, you acknowledge that success is not always immediate, and setbacks & obstacles are the lessons designed for you to learn. Instead of being discouraged by failure, we should be empowered by those experiences as opportunities for growth and improvement. When you have faith in your journey, you will be committed to your goals and take the necessary steps to achieve them, leading to a more fulfilling and rewarding life.

My belief in life is: *"Whatever happened to you, happened for a reason & whoever crossed your path, also crossed for a reason"*

Setting and Achieving Goals

One important aspect of self-empowerment is the ability to set and achieve goals. Without goals, we may feel aimless and uncertain about our future. By setting goals and working towards them, we give ourselves direction and purpose. It's important to remember that goals don't have to be big or complex. They can be as simple as learning a new skill or trying a new hobby. The important thing is that we set them for ourselves and work towards them with determination and focus.

Prioritizing Physical and Mental Health

Another key aspect of self-empowerment is self-care. As a retired registered nurse, Certified Critical Care Nurse (CCRN) and Director of Nurses (DON), I highly recommend prioritizing both your physical and mental health. This includes engaging in regular physical activity, such as walking, running, or yoga, to maintain a healthy weight and reduce t risk of chronic illnesses.

In addition, taking care of your mental health is just as important. Try to make time for relaxation and stress-reducing activities, such as meditation or reading a book. Finally, it's essential to get enough sleep each night to help your body and mind rest and rejuvenate.

Standing Up For Yourself

Self-empowerment also means standing up for ourselves and advocating for our own needs. It's unfortunate that throughout my work life, I've faced discrimination from my male counterparts. Most of the time they would dismiss me without even giving me a chance to share my thoughts or contributions.

It was frustrating but I stood up for myself, my colleagues, my team, and what I believed in on many occasions. One incident I also share in my book is confronting a Prominent Cardiac Surgeon who had a habit of undermining female nurses in my department. Trust me, in that very moment when I verbally faced him, I was shaking in my knees and thought I would get fired right away. It took a lot of courage. He changed his ways and became respectful then after.

Your Self Worth

One important aspect of self-empowerment is developing a strong sense of self-worth. Women often struggle with self-esteem issues, especially in a society that puts so much emphasis on physical appearance and traditional gender roles. But we must remember that our worth is not determined by our looks, our job, or our relationships. We are valuable and deserving of respect simply because we exist as human beings.

Setting Boundaries

Another important aspect of self-empowerment is learning to set boundaries and being able to say no when necessary. As women, we often feel the pressure to be people-pleasers, and to put the needs of others before our own. This, however, can lead to a sense of being burned out, resentment, and a sense of powerlessness. By setting boundaries and saying no when we need to, we are respecting our own needs and desires, and sending a message to others that our time and energy are valuable.

It's important to remember that setting boundaries and saying no doesn't make us selfish or mean. It simply means that we are prioritizing our own well-being and recognizing that we can't be everything to everyone all the time.

Taking Responsibility

Self-empowerment also involves taking responsibility for our own actions and choices. It's easy to blame external factors for our problems and limitations, but this mindset leaves us feeling powerless and stuck. By taking responsibility for our own actions and choices, we are acknowledging that we have the power to make changes and to create the life we choose.

Of course, this doesn't mean that we are solely responsible for our circumstances or that we should blame ourselves for things that are out of our control. But it does mean that we can choose how we respond to our circumstances and how to take action to create a better outcome.

Collaborating With Others

One of my all time favorite quotes is an African proverb that says, "*If you want to go fast go alone. If you want to go far go together.*"

Self-empowerment involves developing a sense of community and connection with others. As women, we are often socialized to compete with one another and tear each other down, but this only serves to hold us back and prevent us from achieving our full potential.

Instead, we must learn to support and uplift one another, recognizing that when one of us succeeds, we all benefit. This can involve building strong relationships with other women, seeking out mentors and role models, and giving back to our communities in meaningful ways.

Prioritizing Your Finances

It is essential for women to have a steady income source and to be able to manage their finances. This means developing financial literacy and being knowledgeable about investments, savings, and budgeting. Having control over your finances can lead to more freedom and independence, giving you the power to make your own decisions without being reliant on others.

Mentoring

One way to empower others is through mentorship. The two factors that contributed to my success in real estate are mentorships and the unwavering determination that I had. I am a member of multiple businesses. CRE Masterminds and Grant Cardone's CRE Club are just two of the many communities that I currently belong to and continue to be empowered by. I've attended and continue to attend real estate conferences, seminars, local meetups and other events regularly. I am always very grateful for all our mentors throughout my journey. Today, I am giving back what I have gathered from my mentorships to my employees, interested strangers, and even to my two sons to become proficient in all matters.

In Conclusion

As women, we are powerful, resilient, and capable of achieving incredible things. By embracing self-empowerment, we can overcome the barriers that hold us back from achieving our goals and aspirations. I love that one reviewer of my book mentioned that my story reminds us of the incredible potential within each of us, and inspires us to pursue our own paths with courage and determination.

Thus, this is to all the women out there. Remember that your self-empowerment is your most valuable asset. Believe in yourself, invest in your education, build a support system, and don't be afraid to take risks. You have the power to achieve anything you set your mind to, and the world needs your unique and individualized talents and contributions. Go out there and make your mark on the world!

Show the world what a fierce and empowered woman can do!

Kelli & Mari Ann Nguyen-Ha

Kelli Nguyen-Ha is a full-time residential & CRE investor for over 14 years. She currently has $10M+ in Assets Under Management, $10M+ as an investor, and $10M+ in single-family homes and commercial real estate transactions completed full cycle. This is all in addition to 20+ years as a business owner, operator, and manager. As a Wall Street Journal & USA Today featured author, Kelli's first book is a love letter to her roots and parents titled: "Immigrant Millionaire: The Story of One Asian Woman Obsessed to Succeed in the Land of Opportunity."

As an investor, Mari Ann has transacted $2M+ CRE deals and $1M+ land deals. She's been a business owner in the beauty industry for 10+ years and has 20+ years of experience in retail business management. Mariann's expertise is in networking and connecting with people. Jennifer has been a successful business owner and an operator in the retail space for over 30 years. Together with their other three sisters as passive partners, FIERCESIX, INC was born and they are on a mission to create a billion-dollar company by 2033 by helping a million families achieve financial freedom through passive income secured by multifamily assets.

Kelli can be reach at

KelliNguyenha.com & *PowerfulFemaleImmigrants.com*

WILL YOU JOIN MY MISSION?

Priscilla Smith, Brazil

It's Friday afternoon and you're done! You don't want to think about work anymore. You've given all your energy, time and tears into a long hard week, and finally the week is over, it's time to go home. You're excited to unwind, relax and spend a nice quiet weekend with your family. Hours later, you are sitting at the kitchen table about to delve into your favorite meal. Then it happens… your stomach sinks into the floor beneath you. Your eyes suddenly open wide as it hits you. On Tuesday you committed to attending an event with a friend on Saturday.

Ahh! How could you forget. You're so tired you don't want to do anything this weekend. Now what? How do you get out of it? You pick up the phone to call your friend. She answers and is super excited for the event. She asks you if you're excited too and after a long pause, you say… um absolutely! What! Why? Why did you say that? Why is it so hard to say no to people?

We do it all the time. We put too much on our plates then we complain because we feel overwhelmed and frustrated. The frustration then turns to anxiety which then translates to having a terrible week, months or perhaps even years. Hear me out, do your conversations sometimes sound like this; man, I'm so tired! There's not enough time in a day, I have so much to do.

But do you? Do you really? The truth is, you don't have a time management problem, you have a people pleasing problem. This phenomenon is a concept that many of us haven't considered when making decisions. You want so badly to have a productive and fulfilling life but often wonder why you're so stressed out. Something has to change, but how? You know you need to put yourself first. It's ok to be selfish. Isn't it? It has to be ok. How can you offer yourself to everyone else when you are falling apart inside? Your cup is empty. There's nothing left, yet you keep tipping the pot to give others every last drop of your being.

By now you're probably wondering why I started my chapter like this. Isn't this supposed to be a book about Powerful Female Immigrants? The women in this book are exactly that, Powerful Female Immigrants. But to be brutally honest, the reason I started my chapter like this is because you and I are not that different. We both want to see the world be a better place, we love powerful movements that push humanity forward, and we want to see others succeed. The truth is most of us find ourselves doing what I described at the start of this chapter but there is a practical way to do what you love and still help others.

Like me, perhaps you've had a difficult past or maybe not, but you root for the little guy. Whatever your story is rest assured you too can be a Powerhouse and help bring change to the world. I believe what makes an immigrant equipped for the job is precisely because of the circumstances they found themselves in at a very young age. See, many of us didn't have a choice when we came to the United States. Nor did we have a choice in the difficulties we endured in order to survive.

From the moment my parents decided to take the leap of faith to migrate to the U.S. my life took a dramatic turn and into absolute chaos.

My parents were born and raised in Sao Paulo, Brazil. My father at a young age knew his destiny was to become a pastor and move to the United States. Three years before I was born, he not only dreamed about it, but he also had an outer body experience in a vision where he was called to go to Albuquerque, New Mexico.

When I was three years old, he left my mother behind in Brazil by herself with seven children. The congregation he led criticized him profusely because of his decision. I mean who does that? What type of man would leave his family behind? He was gone for three whole years. When he returned to pick us all up with all the papers in hand the community was shook. He did it!

Unfortunately, the money ran out and he could not pay the way for his mom to come. A few short weeks after we left my grandmother passed away. My dad was devastated. He says, till this day, she died of a broken heart. The sacrifice my parents made to get us to this country was one I will never understand as now I am happily married with three beautiful children.

However, my life was not always a fairytale the way some would think it is by looking at the things I'm involved with today. You see, before getting to Albuquerque, New Mexico my parents reposed in South Florida for five years. I loved living in the sunshine state, where it's warm year-round and the beaches are beautiful. When we moved to Albuquerque, I was so angry with my parents. I mean for one, it was a desert. Secondly, it was so dark and somber, everything was brown and depressing. Finally, it was teeming with gang violence, murder, drugs, and poverty.

Just weeks after arriving, before we even had an opportunity to settle in, I witnessed my first drive by shooting and murder of a teenage boy. I could not understand what I watched unfold in front of my eyes that morning. Not to mention that no one was outraged or surprised by the ordeal. In fact, no one shed a tear for the little boy laying on that cold concrete floor in front of the local grocery store. My anger immediately grew into a furious wrath. I'd just turned 11 and was in utter shock that my parents would bring our family to this Godforsaken town.

I decided that day that I would eventually end up like that little boy. Dead on the ground trying to escape the very people that promised to be there for him. Like me, he was trapped. What was the point in fighting the madness? I didn't feel heard or seen, by anyone. Nothing I said, no matter how hard I fought, the truth was I wasn't going anywhere. So, I opened my arms out wide and free fell into a deep dark chasm of rage and resentment.

My parents tried their very hardest to provide for us, raising seven children in a new world. The resources for my parents were slim as you can imagine. Living in a new country not knowing one lick of the native language. They kept busy with the ministry and did everything they could to help others. Regrettably, they had no idea that their little girl was addicted to every drug she could lay her little hands on. That led to me getting groomed by local gang members and grown men that only God knows what their intention was with me. When I was 12 years old a friend and I found ourselves hanging out in a strange apartment smoking what we thought was pot with men we barely knew. Suddenly, something told me we needed to get out of there. The *high* felt different! I could barely feel my limbs. Pretending to "feel" normal, I pleaded with my friend to leave. The men did everything they could to keep us there a little while longer, but I insisted.

Looking back now, it was only by the grace of God that we got out of that old apartment. Just minutes later, walking home at 2am, the laced drug hit us so hard we barely made it home. I wondered why those men tried so hard to keep us both from leaving; they planned to gang rape us that night. Despite the escape, it wasn't long after, when I turned 13, I was brilliantly and deceptively groomed and raped. Twice! By someone I looked up to and called friend.

By the time I was 17, we'd lived in a wooden shack that my father built for us. No heat or air conditioning, no running water or bathroom. My mom cooked outside using a tiny one burner propane stove. Later we lived in church buildings and an auto body shop before resting in a small two-bedroom house in the hood. I was still so angry, I knew I'd either end up in prison, dead or trafficked.

What saved me from myself was becoming pregnant shortly after turning 18. I quickly learned I had work ethic and dedicated my life to my new family.

Two decades later I ran into a woman at my kid's school. She asked me if I still liked doing nails. I had no idea what she was talking about. Then she told me she was the old high school principal secretary at my high school. *"You used to come in the office all the time and talk about nails,"* she said. Wow!!! I was stunned. The women had no idea that I was already the CEO of an award-winning nail salon. I never knew I had ambitions at 17, while living in my nightmare. After this encounter I began asking myself, what would have happened if someone came along side me back then and taught me what they knew about the beauty industry?

This was the question that changed EVERYTHING!

I didn't understand why others weren't experiencing the industry like I was, so I started studying why. I hired dozens of aspiring nail techs in my salon and taught them everything I knew about the business. I learned how this industry does something incredible to the psyche of the young women that have experienced trauma. Being touched and being allowed to touch someone else, without the fear of getting hurt was a gamechanger. I've seen it happen repeatedly. As relationships are built with clients, the guards begin to fall, and trust rises to levels that's hard to comprehend. Their confidence quickly emerges to self-worth. It's beautiful!

In 2020, like many of you, Covid devastated families. For me, the stories of hardship young women were facing, living with their abusers amongst financial adversity was eye opening. So, I considered opening a nail technology school to offer them a way out. It wasn't long after that I learned that 50% of the homeless population in New Mexico were teenagers. Amongst many were kids aging out of the foster care system, attempting to escape their abusers or recovering from being sex trafficked. And even if they're not trafficked, they're all at risk. Did you know that when a teenage girl runs away, she is picked up by a human trafficker within 48 hours?

Sex trafficking is a $150 Billion a year industry that makes up more than Coca Cola, Disney, Starbucks, and Netflix combined.

During my research of opening a school I discovered that to enter cosmetology school one only had to be 16 years old. WHOA! I wondered why no one was talking about this. Then it happened, a fire was sparked in me. After years of changing the culture of the nail industry in my salon, I was burdened to do everything in my power to help young women across the globe escape unwanted lifestyles.

For seven years I was using a system I created that allowed me to effectively mentor young women and empower them to find themselves through beauty. What I didn't realize was that with this system, I was operating what would one day become the FIRST nonprofit salon to ever exist. I never expected that the solution to a global problem would 30 years later come out of that little angry girl desperately wanting to be seen.

My book *Unraveling Passion: Confront Your Past To Find Your Future,* tells my story, one I've hidden for 30 years because I was ashamed.

Today I'm here with you, dear reader, because I need your help. There's no shortage of young women that feel stuck, abandoned and can't find a way to escape their unwanted lifestyles. In fact, I'm certain someone's name came to mind when you read that. I believe that through beauty young women across the globe can have access to a tangible solution that will literally save their lives.

In 2021, I founded Passion's Story Inc., the first in the world, a full functioning nonprofit salon that brings communities together to impact a generation of young women that need it the most. I know what you're thinking, how does a nonprofit salon even work?

First, through our scholarship fund, we pay the way for at risk young women to go to beauty school. After they graduate, they will be hired to participate in a 12-month work-study program where they will earn a sustainable income all while building a clientele. During that time, they will have access to on staff counselors and therapists. Local salon owners also known as our *Salon Partners*, will visit us periodically to network, coach and mentor the team. For moms, they will have access to our in-house child learning center that duals as a childcare facility, so they won't have to choose between working or paying for day care again.

After they finish the 12-month program, they will be hired, not based on talent, but based on the connections they made with our *Salon Partners*. There they will continue a thriving career. What many don't realize is that this is an industry that solves problems other industries can't.

It acts as a massive steppingstone to other fulfilling careers. Passion's Story two-generation approach will empower moms to strive even further and break the cycle of poverty.

This is not just a nonprofit; this is a movement. A movement to mobilize the beauty industry and revolutionize the way we impact a generation.

I encourage you to get involved. There's only one way we can have a global impact, and that's for us to work together. Here are some ways you can support.

- Purchase my book, *Unraveling Passion*, all proceeds of the book sales are donated to my nonprofit Passion's Story Inc.
- I am looking for investors to sponsor this project.
- I'm also looking for speaking engagements.

If you know anyone that can help, please email me at priscilla@ paixxao.co. You may also visit www.passionstory.org or www. iamPriscillaSmith.com for more info. I will leave you with this…

Picture a day when your daughter, granddaughter or niece walks up to you and thanks you for seeing them. Hearing them and teaching them and others how to find a way out. Picture a day when you look at yourself in the mirror and are proud for recognizing a need and getting involved with a solution that works.

I pray you will experience the empowerment Passion's Story has on the young women it serves. Will you join my Mission?

Priscilla Smith

After graduating beauty school, I was so put off by two things. First, the subpar service other salons provided to their clients and by the lack of opportunity aspiring nail techs received. I decided to leave behind a 13-years' worth of experience in property management for the nail industry to solve these problems.

In 2016, I opened my salon, and named it after the Portuguese word for passion. As I grew my business, I only hired beauty school graduates; teaching them everything I knew about the business. Within 8 months Paixxão.Co was named the BEST Nail Salon in Albuquerque and has held that title since. To our clients we provide an Elegant and Hygienic Alternative. To our team we provide life transformation through beauty.

I realized early on that many of the talented young women I hired were facing personal challenges that made it difficult for them to succeed. I noticed that the industry offered a unique outlet for them to turn their lives around. Under my guidance and support, they overcame their obstacles and built successful careers.

My salon is not just a business, but a vehicle to empower young women and help them find their self-worth.

For the past seven years, I have dedicated myself to mentoring dozens and helping them become financially independent and creative professionals. Today, I am changing the culture of the beauty industry by introducing the first of its kind, in the WORLD, a nonprofit salon that will help young women escape unwanted lifestyles.

Priscilla can be reach at:

iamPriscillaSmith.com & *PowerfulFemaleImmigrants.com*

FROM 0 TO 1 – WITH THE DEEP BELIEF IN MYSELF AND SUPPORT FROM STRONG LADIES

Qiuxue (Valerie) Yang, China

In my opinion, reaching from 0 to 1 requires a lot of work, but it's probably not the hardest thing ever. However, going from 1 to 0 and starting over again takes not only hard work, but also courage, and perseverance. I wrote this book, because in life, we might experience the failures of going from 1 to 0 over and over again due to things beyond our control, and having the grit to restart is what sets one apart. I was able to do it with the firm belief in myself and the guidance of many strong female figures in my life and I want to spread that spirit.

In this chapter, I will talk about my journey in America where I studied at 4 different schools and finally got into the best program in quantitative finance. I moved across the globe from China to the United States, from the east coast to the West coast, then eventually landed my dream job in wealth management. It also talked about my personal life, and how I navigated through divorce and built my life again, thriving and feeling more fulfilling than ever through relationshipbuilding, and finding my true passion. It touches on how I built my career and overcome the difficulties of being minorities and found my edge and bloomed. I went through the process from being

0 to 1 over and over again. All of this cannot be done without the inspiration and support of the strong female figures in my life. I just want to share my story and hopefully you will find one or two pieces of thoughts or experience useful.

Coming to America - the spring chicken

It's funny whenever people learn that I came to the US by myself at age 18 without knowing anyfriends or relatives, they are usually very surprised and said: you must be very brave. I usually nodded along politely and thanked them for their compliment. But truthfully, I didn't feel that I really deserved that compliment, not because I am not worthy, but because I truly wasn't scared or worried at the time. To me, it was rather a fun adventure! The intention was very simple at the **time** I wanted to receive the best college education, and it must be on the other side of the world. I wanted to leave China, leave my comfortable home and explore the world on my own and discover what the land of freedom looks like. At that time, not many people that I know have studied abroad, but I have read stories about kids studying at schools like Stanford: they would work on projects with people from different parts of the world, lying on the grass and reading books in the warm sunny afternoon and eventually working in cities like the big apple, London or Tokyo. All of this just seems so appealing and glamorous to me and really set fire in my heart. So when my mom asked me: Do you want to study abroad? I said yes without hesitation.

Now you can say, I was young and naive and there is a Chinese saying for that "初生牛犊不怕虎" meaning: the newborn cow doesn't fear the tiger, mostly because it doesn't know yet. I think that is partly true. I was a young, energetic, and full A student who is loved by teachers and fellow students. I had a lot of confidence that I could make my beautiful dream of studying abroad by myself come true. I wasn't thinking too much about the difficulties and unknowns. In addition, I am also deeply influenced by my mom. She is a strong lady who is a business owner with a full sense of humor. I have never heard her complaining about difficulties in her life or blaming others. My childhood memories are that we always laughed together because she tells good jokes and we would dream together about what it would be like if I go to college in another city or how cool it would be if I become a talk show host one day! Her confidence and belief in me made the young me believe in myself without a doubt.

Now, I might be a romantic at heart, but I know when to be realistic and practical. I studied economics and mathematics for my undergraduate degree. I know I wanted to study finance in grad school and having a solid foundation of quantitative skills is critically important. I also transferred from a small community college in Pennsylvania to Purdue to get a better academic environment and more exposure to peers in the Engineering and qualitative fields. That was my first move in the States, from the east coast to the Midwest. I feel like I was a little bit closer to my goal.

As I progressed my study at Purdue, I quickly realized that having just an economic degree wasn't enough to get me into a big investment company in cities like NYC or the Bay area, and I can't go to a top MBA program because they require working experience. To make matter worse, my status as an international student pretty much prevented me from having just an "ok" job such as an office clerk or fast food worker as I will need a working visa and sponsorship to work in the US and only big companies can offer that. Therefore,

I know that I need to have a graduate degree in a competitive field that not everyone can study. I did a lot of research and found a field called "financial engineering" – it's a degree that prepares financial professionals called "Quant" who work on Wall Street and build financial models for stock options and risk management. It's the earlier version of now called "data analytics" or "business analytics". It was very appealing to me as I always feel like the econ and business classes at the undergrad level are very concept and theory-based, without much data and quantitative support. Therefore, I took many math and statistics, and computer programming classes to prepare myself for my study in financial engineering in grad school. Those classes weren't easy, but I enjoyed them a lot. Eventually, I got my bachelor's degree in Economics with minors in math and stats at Purdue and got into both USC and UCLA. I chose the financial engineering program at UCLA, which is one of the top MFE programs in the US. In my fourth year of living in the States, I moved from the Midwest to the west coast and was one step closer to my dream.

The dream begins in LA

I have never imagined that I would ever live in LA or even California because it always seems too good to be true. I remembered the sunshine and palm trees when I had a layover at LA airport on my way to Philadelphia. It was just a blimp of good memories back then, but now it came true. I was excited, anxious, and a little scared, but ultimately very happy. Classes at UCLA were hard, and probably the most challenging compared to all other schools I have studied at. I can say I never rested one full day while I was there. I didn't even know what the campus really looked like until after I graduated and had the time to walk around. I would spend all my time at the library at Anderson business school and working on projects. We use to envy MBA students as they have so much time networking and going out. I still remember that I got sick from a cold during the final's week, with cramps from my period, but still needed to prepare for the exams, work on my project and study for an interview, and I cannot mess up any one of them. Oh I was so exhausted that I cried. But I soldiered through and finished all of these tasks one by one! I think that experience really gave me the confidence and prepared me to survive under any stressful circumstances because I still don't think I have worked in any high-pressure environment that will measure up to my grad school life. In the end, I finished my degree and got my full-time offer on the day of graduation while my parents were visiting me! One of the highlights of my life!

But only I know how hard I had worked on not only finishing the degree but also getting a job. I knew I wanted to work in the asset management industry, so when the interview opportunity came, I actually read through several research papers, and made notes on all of them about the best methods of pricing financial assets, and what improvement one could do. When I presented that to my now boss at the interview, he was very impressed, probably because he had never seen any candidates bring research papers to an interview. Not surprisingly, I got the job. I think at that time I can say I got from 0 to 1 on a beginner level.

I am lucky that I have supportive parents who are behind all my decisions and support me financially. They are the reason why I dare to dream and able to achieve many things. When I told my mom that I am jumping schools from USC to UCLA because they have better programs, but it will be doubling the cost, she said "do it!" without hesitation and paid all my tuition and living cost. My then boyfriend who later became my husband was also very supportive emotionally, he would talk me through many problems on the daily basis and was by my side on every decision. He and his parents actually helped me move across the country to study at UCLA. I am forever thankful for that. At last, I thank myself, who had the guts and determination to figure all that out at such a young age. Maybe it didn't feel much at the time, but i want to say to my young self: Job well done, girl! I am proud of you.

Building my career: aiming for the 1

I am lucky enough that wealth management is my first job, and later on, became my career. I also happen to work with a group of caring and genuine people. My bosses are like my parents and always look after me. But if I ask myself, why do I choose this to be my career, I think it is the influence of my role model - my mom. She was a successful businesswoman who ran an import/export company in China. She was at the top of her field and that gave us comfortable lifestyles. But what sets her apart was her vision of investing. She saw opportunities in the real estate market in China 25 years ago and invested in a hotel development project that was a rare opportunity at the time. Then she was patient enough to wait for 20 years to let it grow, then sold half of it when the market peaked and invested the proceeds in bonds and CDs. she might not realize what she was doing was called financial planning and asset allocation (giving it financial terms). But she was very intuitive, observant, and decisive – She is a savvy investor. She planned ahead and invested in long-term real estate when everyone else was just putting their money in savings or some stocks. She then sells them ruthlessly when it reaches her target valuation,   and invested in bond and money markets funds to plan her retirement. This gives her the lifestyle she deserves to have, and I never have to worry about the well-being and financial life of my parents. Therefore, I went into this business knowing I am helping build future for families. My prudent and diligent work on how to build the appropriate financial plan and the asset allocation decision on when to overweight stocks over bonds or real estate over commodities is important, because it is directly correlated with their lifestyle and their happiness.

However, moving up in this career isn't easy. In the end, this business is about people and relationship management. I was a first-generation immigrant minority woman who didn't know anyone. English isn't my first language, and I can't understand half of the jokes when people talk about sports (very common in the financial industry). When I first started, I honestly didn't know if I would survive or if this was the right thing for me. At the time, almost everyone in this industry is Caucasian male in their 50s. This doesn't represent me at all and I felt out of the place. Now many people at this point probably will give up and tell themselves that they could never make it because their ethnicity, gender, or other factors can never be changed. But that's not how I was raised. My parents always told me "if you are gold, you will shine no matter where you are" and I truly believe in that. So I started approaching the Chinese CPA community and asked them if they could refer some business to me, and something did happen. I still remember that the CPA who referred my first client told me that

"I know you are young, but I can see the passion in your eyes, and you have a very experienced team behind you, so I trusted you." I was 27 at the time, and my first ever client was a Chinese businessman who owns a food factory in China. I was thrilled!

At the same time, I was working very hard on building up my own referral network of CPAs, attorneys, insurance agents etc. At the end of the day, we want to have a team of experts to serve our clients, like an early model of the virtual family office (VFO). Later on, I realized that if I just focused on the Chinese community, I would be limiting myself because that's still a small part of the population. What about focusing on people who have similar interests and backgrounds? That really opened up my mind and vision! The millennials love entrepreneurship and creating things of their own because that gives us a sense of accomplishment. I see the trend that more and more young people start working for themselves. As they are approaching the point of selling their companies, comprehensive financial planning is needed to make sure their liquidity event is tax efficient and their profit is maximized. A team of M&A attorneys, CPAs, and investment advisors is built to work together to make sure the process goes smoothly and the appropriate financial plan is built. I want to be part of that and witness the growth of a company and how it eventually got handed over to the right person/ entity. It's proven that our financial planning work has been crucial to the liquidity event and our asset allocation work helps growing assets. This is very exciting and I feel very fortunate that my work is adding value to something that means a lot to clients. As of now, I haven't achieved the 1 that I dreamed of yet, but I firmly believe I will get there someday, because I believe I can always do better!

Love and relationship: From 1 to 0

At one point, I almost felt that I got everything figured out. I was married to my college sweetheart and we were together for 8 years. Our relationship was very stable, and we were by each other's side for everything, both good and bad. What's more, we were both doing well in our careers and everything was smooth sailing. I firmly believed that I will be with this person forever as we went through so many things in our adult life that it almost felt like we grew up together. So when he just told me that he couldn't continue with me anymore, because he has no feelings left for me, I was in shock. To this day, I still don't understand the exact reason why he left as we don't really have fights or arguments much. Sure, we no longer have the sparkles or butterflies that new couples do, but things were working from my view. I begged him to stay. He wouldn't change his mind whatsoever and then moved out very quickly. He did list a list of things that I failed to do and things he didn't like, which we have never talked about before. It really felt like a nuclear bomb and my heart was broken into million pieces. I felt blind-sighted and betrayed. Those were the darkest days of my life. Hurt by the person you trusted the most was the worst. Days of insomnia and seeking answers for what happened exactly and what I did wrong eventually led to anxiety attacks. I felt my life was falling apart and I didn't know what to do about it. I went back to China for three weeks to be with my parents. It was good to be surrounded by family and friends, which helped distract me from my sadness. But I soon realized that I don't belong there anymore. My real home is the one in LA.

After coming back to LA, I started therapy sessions for the first time in my life, and really had the time to process my pains, and reflected on what went wrong with my relationship. It was a long and hard process.

Many back-and-forth, self-doubts, and crying nights. Eventually, about 5 months after our separation, I moved passed the initial heartbreak and trying to live life again. But then the new challenge came along. I felt that I got nothing left when he left and it was just myself in the house. I had a lot of friends, but no one was close enough that I could just pick up the phone and cry about my divorce. I don't have family in the States that I could visit on the weekend or holidays so I feel belong. I used to spend all my free time with him and his family and they essentially became my family in the States. But unfortunately, all of that was gone with him. I felt like I was trying to walk again, but half of my arms and legs were cut off. It was a helpless time and the pain of growing was felt vividly.

I was very confused at that point: was my life prior to the divorce a dream and unreal? Why did my life go from 1 to 0 again? Where do I go from here? Fortunately, I was never an anti-social person, and I reached out to my friends. My girlfriends who weren't even super close to me at the time came along and opened their arms. They spent hours with me on the phone when I needed to talk or have a shoulder to cry. They took me hiking, to church, and on trips. During that time, I learned a lot about them, on a much deeper level - their struggles, and perspectives on life. I felt bad that I didn't get to know them so deeply before. Later on, my mom was worried about me, so she lived with me for 3 months and we traveled to many places together including Portland, Bahamas, and Hawaii. That was the longest time we spent together after I became an adult. Slowly I started healing with the love and support of family and friends.

I think at that point I started finding peace and was ready to face the new chapter of my life. Although the sadness still came all of sudden and caught me off guard sometimes, I don't have to find endless activities to fill my daily routine, or always hang out with friends to kill the loneliness. I started re-discovering my hobbies, like practicing piano again, a hobby I did for 10 years, and forgot about after I came to the US. I improved my skills and had concerts with my friend Iris, and went to an International competition in Paris with her. A memory I will never forget. I started to appreciate piano in a deeper way and it eventually became a daily routine for me. I learned to surf during the pandemic and was able to catch some waves. I am still no expert, but it made me feel like a superwoman in the ocean! I also picked up skiing, a sport I probably would never try before, but I actually enjoy it. And guess what, I started dating again, uncomfortable at first, but I enjoy meeting new people, getting connected, and having some fun in my life. Oh, man, I finally felt alive and thriving again and not afraid of expressing my needs and desire, something I have lost in touch with for a while due to being content and stuck in my comfort zone. the process has been slow and muddy, but i can start seeing the light at the end of the tunnel. I can say with 100% confidence that I have grown in that one year after divorce 5x faster than my previous years, and I really think I have become a better person. I have more compassion for others, especially divorced women and single moms. I learned that in life, nothing is really that certain, and counting our happiness on one single thing or person is dangerous. So I started consciously building relationships, especially my supporting group, and giving them care and help when possible. I started connecting people, and giving back to the community. For example, helping UCLA students when they need career advice because I was there before. I wouldn't say this divorce is a good thing or wish it happen to anybody. But I came out becoming a better person, a person with deep compression for others and a firm belief to myself that I can do it.

Recovering from the divorce and building a new life hasn't been easy, and i don't wish it to happen to anybody. But if things go from 1 to 0 again. I believe I have the courage to start over and thrive from it. I think the firm belief in myself and the love and support from family and friends are the most important things that help me go through the hardest days. I still remember during the darkest days of my life, a sentence from my grandma always popped up in my head: "I can't let others kills me!" (by kill, she means push down). When I spent my childhood time with her, she used to say this in a very determined, but also funny way when she faces difficulties as if she almost look down to the challenges. Somehow this sentence stuck with me and eventually became my mantra and a deep belief. In addition, I am fortunate to have many strong female figures that guide me through difficult times and teach me to be resilient. My mom is always my biggest fan, and always believes in me and gives me the best advice a daughter could ask for regardless of career or personal life. I have a group of girlfriends whom I dearly love and admire. These are doctors, lawyers, programmers, and businesswomen who are there for me through ups and downs and create beautiful memories together. My life blooms because of them.

In the end, I just wanted to emphasize the point that we will always try our best to make it from 0 to 1, whether be our career, relationships, or personal growth. But if things ever go south and we are back to where we were, we could always smile to ourselves and say it confidently: Let's start over and we can do it again!

Qiuxue (Valerie) Yang

Valerie is from Tianjin, China, and moved to the United States to pursue her college degree when she was 18. She graduated from UCLA with a master degree in financial engineering. She also graduated from Purdue University with a bachelor's degree in economics with a minor in mathematics.

Currently, Valerie works as a senior director of investment at Summa Group, the top wealth management team at Oppenheimer in the nation with assets under management of $2.5 billion. The Summa Group serves affluent families and caters to their complex needs in planning and investment management. Valerie is responsible for investment research, portfolio management and developing planning strategies. She works closely with client fiduciaries including CPAs, estate planning lawyers and business managers in order to make holistic investment decisions for clients. Valerie's team works with entrepreneurs, senior executives, fiduciaries and founders that have recently experienced or are about to experience a life-changing financial event such as inheritance, stock sales and closely held business sales. She plays an integral role within the core advisory team that deals with these pre and post-liquidity events and develops planning strategies. In addition, Valerie is a member of the Los Angeles Financial Planning Association (FPA) and holds the Certified Financial Planner (CFP) designation from the Certified Financial Planner Board of Standards, Inc

She currently resides in Los Angeles, California In her free time, Valerie enjoys playing the piano, surfing, hiking, and traveling to different parts of the world. She performs at concerts at times and competed at an International piano competition in Paris. She loves art and is a regular visitor to museums and galleries. She is a foodie who loves cooking and dining at different restaurants with her friends.

Valerie can be reach at:

linktr.ee/valerie.yang & *PowerfulFemaleImmigrants.com*

ENLIGHTENMENT THROUGH A MURKY PATH

Susie Mosqueda, Mexico

Nor the muddy long lines of the fields nor the harsh stinging words that come with racism, discrimination, language barriers, cultural stigmas, illness, death, and a toxic marriage brought down this fierce resilient Aztec warrior. At this very moment I am in my recently remodeled backyard drinking a glass of Moscato, my favorite wine. It is incredible how far I've come all the way from those long lines in the fields of Mexico where I enjoyed harvesting cucumbers, to an elegant, sophisticated patio in the United States, to a fulfilling life. I can't believe it!!! I will never forget where that little girl came from, without shoes. What she went through, and how proud I am of her courage and her accomplishments. Moreover, of her resilience, determination which continues supporting her on an inward journey of self discovery of her highest limitless potential. I will always embrace my ancestors' relentless spirit. SHE will never be defeated.

Departing to "El Norte"

It was right after Christmas eve when my father said to my mom, two younger brothers and I, a teenager , *"Empaquen dos blusas, dos pantalones y ya. Nos vamos mañana.*" (Pack 2 shirts, 2 pants. That's it, we leave tomorrow.") And just like that, in the blink of an eye, my family and I left to embark on our trip to the USA. A trip we had been waiting for a long time. A journey we envisioned to improve our lives, just like other people who have been there before us have done it.

Pero, What does this mean and feels to me, to a teenager!? It's like, *¡¡¡en serio!!!* (seriously!!!) I left my colorful country, Mexico right at a point in my life when a female human is starting to develop her personality. To decide who she is based on her surroundings, and depends a whole lot on the community around her to support her through that process. Well, for me that was long gone once we got on that bus.

While I was super excited about going to "el norte," thinking my dreams of becoming a professional singer and dancer would come to fruition, I felt a huge sorrow. I mean, it was Christmas for God sake, and Christmas in Mexico for me is everything. It's part of me. On the bus, I had plenty of time to contemplate who I was up until that very moment and the uncertainty I was about to face, which I had no idea of the magnitude of. See, working in the fields I already knew there was greatness for me to accomplish. No idea on the HOW or the WHAT or the WHY, but a strong intuitive knowing. Although I was leaving during my favorite season, I was extremely excited and scared at the same time. Finally, there was hope that all of these desires would come true. But oh gush, the pain. At what cost.

I did not know I must be detached from who I was to become who I wanted to be or who I was destined to become. My friends, who I grew up with and went to school with. Shared countless memories with, were not there no more. I could not just tell my mom that I was visiting a friend anymore. All my family, my roots, my traditions, dinner with my aunts, the fun work in the fields, everything that I identified myself with, suddenly was gone, DEATH. A world inside out changed without a warning and to be honest, It was until later that I found out the damage and benefits of this Christmas migration journey. I cannot even imagine what this encompasses to my two little brothers.

But I was delighted and grateful that my father could bring us all to the United States, regardless of what this really meant. Deep inside me, I could sense it was going to be better than one room for five people and no shoes.

The Wall

I am in the United States, aaajuaa!!! Now what? It's winter time, trees are dead, my thinking about it says, why do people still have these dead trees up? Cut them down. Keep in mind, back in Guanajuato, Mexico, trees never lose their leaves completely throughout the seasons. This is just one of the little changes I went through. Carajo, who would have thought how enduring and exhausting, both psychologically, emotionally, and physically this experience was going to be. Almost traumatizing. Does anybody talk about this? What a cultural shock on every level one can possibly think of. First of all, this world was extremely out of my league. I did not know how to speak a word in English but the word *"no"*, I was totally foreign to the school system and there was nothing in place to guide me or to help my parents navigate it. The dating arena, completely strange, even among Mexicans, oh and let's add racism and discrimination something I had never heard of before. *¡Oh cielos,* I hit a huge wall!*

My self-confidence went downhill instantly on the first interaction with other people at the store. My dad, so proud to have all of his family together with him, which could be perceived kilometers away in his smile, the way he walked, how he talked to us about the huge opportunity ahead of us, took us to the grocery store. Believe me, as we crossed the door I was stupefied. My jaw dropped beyond the floor and I am not exaggerating. I never do. What a humongous store. Nothing in comparison to my Tio's Jose's little grocery store. Nobody talked to me about these little big differences I was about to encounter myself with in this new place. And then thirty years ago, there was consistently a lady greeting you by the entrance of the store, well now I know that's what the lady did. Back then, I froze, became intimidated, ashamed, small, I shrunk, just smiled and never talked about it until now.

I remember vividly the first day in January of 1994 when I first rode a school bus. A school bus? What is that? I walk to school! It was 5:00 AM. It was still very dark, something really unusual. We were the first ones from "Casa de la Esperanza, " an apartment complex, to be picked up, to have a long couple hours route to school and arrive there around 7:30AM.

At my classes, my white classmates would laugh at me about my English pronunciation. Such was the case that it took me years to feel confident enough to say the word "sheet" for paper, again. There were experiences when even my own people let me down and did not help me with something like finding where my classes were. At points, I cried, but I did not know if it was because of my period or because I missed my Mexico *"lindo y querido."* How to know? I mean there are counselors and psychologists who specialize in whatever, but is there anybody who studies the impact of almost, and sometimes forcely moving to another country? The psychology process behind this? Finally, in college originally I wanted to pursue computer programming. However, I was still on the low spectrum of English. Moreover, did not know how to solicit financial assistance, how to communicate, *NADA*. So I quitted on this first attempt. ¡*Que dicen*! So many things I want to say. That wall, the unknown school system designed not for people like me, was not easy to go through.

Foggy Walk

Dragging shoes of shame, of fear, of desolation as I walk on the streets of loneliness barefooted. Confusion and disorientation invaded my whole identity. For instance, when I went to the doctor, I was no longer Susana, I became Susanna, Suzzanne, and many other people I did not recognize. See, growing up, "los gueros", white people were seen and treated like royalty. I believe this generational belief came from the era of colonization. So, the way this affected me is, I felt that I was not worth to ask for help or to even speak. On top of not knowing the language, I carried the burden of oppression of my ancestors. Therefore, being so unaware of my true self and potential and value, I did not proclaim my name, Susana Mosqueda. I did not know how to defend or protect the beauty of my own culture.

Throughout the years many events happened. I got married to a narcissist, following the crowd, had two lovely sons, I got seriously ill with ulcers colitis for almost twenty years , I had non-hodgkin's disease cancer stage four, and technically died at the age of 29ish after my intestine was perforated during a routine colonoscopy procedure (due to extreme psychological and emotional abuse). Who am I really?

That was the question that pounded my mind for years, ever since my name was not my name anymore and I have given permission for that to happen. Oh cielos, I had to admit the responsibility of giving conscious or unconscious permission for all of this to happen or even created it myself with my unaware imagination.

Who am I REALLY? An agonizing cultural battle was consuming the little faith and hope left in me. Between not understanding my evolution as a woman out of the "rancho" my little town, in comparison to the experienced highly educated woman with an university degree, adding a punitive, oppressive marriage, it felt like the wings I once had as a little girl without shoes, were tight up with thorn wire. And I did not know how to liberate myself. I had nobody who could understand what I was going through. How to get out of this iron cage? I felt ashamed of who I was because I did not know how to show to the world, most importantly, I did not know how to show up for MYSELF.

The Eagle Has Awaken

And it was necessary to die so I could live. Because just after death is when one can truly find the space for the authentic SELF. Not in body, but in spirit. As I found myself in front of a peaceful light, I could see that little girl in Mexico harvesting her favorite fruit in a muddy, difficult to walk line, cucumbers. Her smile is brighter than the sun itself. Her belief in herself, her faith and determination are indestructible. She envisions greatness and trusts that she will make it happen. She knows already, she is not alone. Our ancestors are there to guide her, to protect her. She just has to STOP and listen.

Now, after DEATH, I remember who I am, I am an Aztec Resilient Warrior, never defeated. This version of me is a combination of the magnificent skills I inherited from my ancestors, from my mother, from my tías, from the land I grew up at, nature, my past, and now my present. I am an unshakable resilient woman of God. My given name is Susana Mosqueda, if you are my friend you can call me Susi.

The process of cleansing the accumulated mess throughout years of resistance to acculturation, resistance to continue emulating every woman in my town of getting married, having children and doing what your husband says, forgetting about you; it was the most excruciating pain I have ever endured. The hardest part was to detach from everything, every single belief, label, TODO that I had identified myself with up until that point. I had to kill the old toxic version of me in order to create space for the new. Nobody knew what I was feeling inside. No coach, mentor, just me and my intuition took this inward dark shadow journey. I faced DEATH again!

The emptiness which is mainly expressed as loneliness, was real. But I did not go back. After reconnecting to my inner brilliance, all I can feel and see is JOY, fulfillment. I am so proud of that little Mexican girl from "el rancho" without shoes who dared to take the courageous decision to break the chains of cultural stigmas and layers of suffering.

Susie Mosqueda

I currently hold a Masters degree in Multicultural Education with an endorsement in Linguistic Diverse Instruction. I am the Executive Director of RTE Academy for Alphas. I am the founder and CEO of IDENTIDAD Leadership Academy for Youth. Most importantly, I am the creative creator of my own fate. I am the descendant of the resilient Aztec women from whom I've learned to stand tall, with a humble pride of my origins. Disconnected from everything to stay connected to everything, SELF. To embrace change, death as part of evolution, of growth.

Susie can be reach at:

linktr.ee/resiliency & *PowerfulFemaleImmigrants.com*

WHAT DO YOU DO?

Migena Agaraj, Albania

A favorite question of mine. It works as an engine to perfect the answer each time we hear it. It makes us think it makes us smile. It makes us feel important and creativity goes to work, sometimes at full speed, sometimes slowly to provide the best answer possible. Very rarely, we hear one sentence when we hear this question being asked. At least this is my experience. For the most part, it starts with a few sentences, and it turns into a paragraph and very often the answer leads to a follow up call because not enough time is there to fully know what one does. I love when I ask others what they do because I see their facial expressions, their body language changes, and I begin to wonder, are they happy with what they do? Are they passionate? Do they know what they really do, or they just have an idea. Therefore, I look forward to asking this question and being asked, especially lately. I'll tell you more in a little Why? For now, let's go back to the beginning of my journey as a bestselling author.

It took a while for the dream to reappear, and I accepted the opportunity and wrote my first chapter in June 2022 and in August 2022 the book was launched.

It is true that the universe conspires when we show up for ourselves.

"Powerful Female Immigrants" Volume One

Spring 2022 I was traveling back to New York, and received a text from my friend Michael, who is a book publisher. "I am working on a book collaboration with Powerful Female Immigrants, and I'd like for you to be a part of it." I saw the text and smiled, and my response was, "lol, this is Migena., you must have sent this message to me by mistake"

Mike responds quickly and he reassures me he has the right person and I wanted to jump off my seat. Could it be that my dream I had locked in a drawer was creating emotions. I didn't know then why I was feeling that way, but I do know now and in fact, I am sure, my dream was cheering from us. Since I was a little girl, I always wanted to write books. I grew up in a big family. Every time we gathered, we would go around the tables telling jokes and sharing stories. My parents always told me and my brother stories from their childhood, youth and their ancestors. I would be transported each time and imagine every single one of these sacred stories belonged in books that the world would have the privilege to read. When I moved to the United States in 2003, I will be very honest, I forgot about this dream as I was too busy being taken by Life.

It took a while for the dream to reappear, and I accepted the opportunity and wrote my first chapter in June 2022 and in August 2022 the book was launched.

It is true that the universe conspires when we show up for ourselves.

"Where are you from? "Was the title of my chapter on the book collaboration, "Powerful Female Immigrants" Volume One, Sounds familiar, right? If you are reading my chapter, you know you are on volume two of a collaboration with other phenomenal powerful Female Immigrants from all over the world, who are continuing to inspire greatness. Volume one has brought magic into my life on a global scale on so many levels. Becoming an author gave life to more than one dream. A story is not just a story. The story is Hope for a little girl who dares to dream, for a little boy to understand his mother better, for her husband to get to know their significant other from a different light, for a friend or even a stranger to apply the messages into their lives.

I am honored to be here again on this Vol.2. It's a gift and responsibility which I take very seriously.

"Clubhouse"

During the pandemic in 2021, I downloaded a social app called Clubhouse, which a connection known as 10k cards, recommended and there I spent most of my time when I was not working. This app gave me the opportunity to connect on a global level. People from all over the world, at least ten million users communicated with one another in real life 24/7 for years. I made friends, discovered new books, learned about the power of voice, cleared words I never heard before, connected with thousands of people, met hundreds in real life and collaborated with dozens. One of them was Michael from Beyond Publishing. On this app, I began to follow Grant Cardone. I had no idea who he was. However, every time he would be on the app, thousands would join. I was curious to know why and how he drew crowds. Over time I got it. Because he could talk to anyone regardless of where people were from, and I liked that because I also love to speak to anyone in the world regardless of their walk of life, profession, age or gender.

"The power of Ask"

One day, I decided to send Grant a message on Clubhouse and ask him to help me buy a ticket to his sold-out Real Estate Summit in December 2021. I knew I had to be there. I didn't know why and wanted to follow my inner voice. I realized I was feeling content for a long time and this feeling, I learned, was very dangerous. I decided to save myself and get out of this comfort zone. Are you wondering what happened with the message to Grant? He did respond! After the response, I had to show up at the event. A multi-multi-millionaire, international speaker, best-selling author, billion-dollar real estate guru, number one salesperson in the world, stopped what he was doing at that given moment, and claimed full responsibility for a stranger. He showed up for me. I had no excuse not to show up.

"Get up, dress up and show up"

December 2021, I am in Aventura at a three-day summit. It was nothing like I imagined. I had low expectations I guess because I wanted to avoid the disappointment from the outcome, this time it was a game changer for me. Grant shared so openly, and with generosity and I had zero excuses not to be successful. A sense of guilt took over me that I did not feel accomplished enough, if there is such a thing as enough… There were moments where I felt I had disrespected my family and all their sacrifices. They left everything behind to bring my brother and myself to the land of opportunities. There I was sitting on the VIP seat with hundreds of questions. Then it got even better. People got up and shared their stories of successes and failures and how they got back up. The entire time. I'm thinking: if that was me, imagine how many lives I would help and bring value to. I felt selfish that I didn't take massive action a long time ago. I know regret won't serve us any good, yet there I was, regretting not listening to my mother all the times she encouraged me to dream bigger, to do more, to be more. I remember one day I told her that my friend David, a strategic partner for the company I was working for, told me I would be president one day. My mom smiled, shook her beautiful head full of unparalleled wisdom and said to me: Not President, you will be CEO. My response to her was a laugher in disbelief. An accomplishment so far and difficult to reach. I was wrong once again, and my mother was right AGAIN!

On day three at the summit, I signed up for Grant Cardone 's Real Estate Club where for a full year I would meet on a zoom call with Grant and hundreds of professionals mainly from the United States. I knew I had to be in their presence.

"Massive Actions"

I decided to resign from my six-figure job as Director of Business Development and commit to the unknown journey. On a phone call with a friend, I stated "life is no longer going to take me. Watch me where I take life."

I began to travel and explore what else was there for me to be a part of. It is very true that no one can accomplish anything alone, however, it takes one person to decide to take massive action and that is you. No matter how much everyone will contribute to your success, it begins with you. And that December, I gave myself permission to be more, do more, have more.

It was very scary to resign my job, to start 2022 with zero income and no plan. I also knew, I had the biggest support system in the world, my family. My parents and my brother who believe in me and supported me. There is no way I am going to let them down. They are the fuel. I know for a fact, there was no going back on my decision to take massive action and continue to build Migena. This action would contribute toward the strength needed to be a stronger source for everyone in my life who I knew and was going to meet from then on.

"Think Bigger"

At the summit, I met Brad who also had joined the Real Estate Club. We decided to get to know each other better and become partners. A few weeks after we met, he presented a deal to the club and Grant Cardone liked it. He offered to help us buy a multifamily deal. We were very grateful and excited for this once in a lifetime opportunity. A week later, we were on a zoom call with Grant, and I had to pinch myself a few times to make sure this was real and happening for us. A month later Brad and I raised almost 3 million dollars in 20 minutes from the members of the club for the deal.

This is what I wanted to do moving forward: raise capital, find deals, connect with people, create generational wealth for all of us, contribute and influence the world, one person at a time. There is a saying that goes like this." I can trust you with my life, but I don't know if I can trust you with my money." Every time I pick up the phone to present deals, I looked forward to building with the person on the other line trust through my experience. I was inspired to bring smiles during zooms or at coffee meetings because the question is always a constant "what do you do ".

"POP ~ People Over Profit"

I remember how scary it was when I made my first investment in the Cardone capital as a limited partner for 348 units in Miami. Another big step towards generational wealth creation. It started with one decision. This one decision would serve me and my network. When you are a consumer first you can relate to the other person a little bit better. At the end of the day, the relationship with money differs, how we earn, how we spend, how we invest, determines our character and personality. I learn by doing and as a result I felt more confident sharing with others the positive outcomes and the risks involved with every single investment. This includes investing on a ticket to attend an event. I know how it feels for me, yet the same amount and experience feels very different for someone else because of how they earned that same amount. My mission has always been POP (I came up with it :)) People Over Profit. The knowledge learned so far would be applied exactly with the highest regard on the relationship, not profit.

"Consistency is Key"

The more I traveled the more I wanted to travel. Not only by plane, car or foot. I love traveling virtually. My first podcast interview was presented to me by a 13-year-old boy from Algeria named Mohammed. He's a brilliant young man and as I say he is 13 going on

2000 years old. His wisdom is unparalleled for his age. His questions were profound. One of my favorites was: "How do you feel now that you know yourself?" My response was: "Every morning I look forward to getting to know myself better through the experiences." There is so much beauty in the unknown. I decided to be consistent and raise my hand and ask every time for the opportunity even when not available yet. I understood the power of consistency over a decade ago. I bought tickets to attend events and always showed up. Many still wonder how I know so many people. I promise you it is not because I am more special than anyone else or that I have more knowledge. It is because I showed up consistently as my true self. The key to consistency is not only to show up it is how you show up. Invest to sit down and learn from others. Invest to stand up for others to know you. Either way it's an investment in yourself, the most important investment of all.

"Express to influence"

For anyone who will have the opportunity to read this book and get to my chapter. I hope my experiences shared here speak to you and inspire you. We are blessed to be alive. Keep in mind that how you embrace the blessings determines the outcome of your lives. Say yes to an opportunity, to an invitation to do something that you never imagined you would be able to do. Grace yourself with acceptance. Be flexible like water, be understanding, compassionate, loving, caring, giving, daring, dreaming, and what your heart desires. If I have touched even one life, mission accomplished. I pray you pay it forward. Go back to your dream drawer and bring them to life. It is never too late.

"Say YES!"

I said yes to Michael's invitation to be an author, with dozens of women who are phenomenal in their own ways they inspire me to do better. Their stories are beautiful, and I am blessed to be in their presence. That first opportunity created the legacy to continue. On Vol. 2 I invited over 70 women to share their stories, and 20 are authors in this vol. The Book led to interviews in Albania. Hundreds of Albanians from all over the world reached out to me. It is indeed a feeling I cannot describe but all I can say is I am humbled, grateful and honored that they chose to hear my story.

I said yes to Adam and Rasha to be the TV host at the premiere for the Red-Carpet event of America's Real Deal, the first investment TV Show through crowdfunding. They believed in me without even knowing me. Today I'm a TV host and associate Director and part of the team for the TV show. I feel privileged to discover businesses in America, invite celebrities, mentors, and icons to be on the show. Collectively through organized efforts, we are working towards changing one life at a time, one business at a time, one family at a time. One of the best rewards and a thank you back to my ancestors, my family, my mother, my father, my brother, who continue to support me in pursuing my dreams. I owed it to that little girl, who pretended her hairbrush was a microphone and had imaginary interviews on her show. I wonder how she knew this dream would be a reality. I don't want to think about how she would feel, if I kept that pure and innocent dream locked in a drawer. One thing is for sure, she dared to dream BIG, and I honor us today.

I said he must be featured in a global women's magazine. I love sharing my story for the ones that need even a spark of hope. That little girl was waiting for this dream as well. This was no longer a dream through TV and Imagination.

I said yes to the opportunity to join the Real Estate Club. I can say that I am a real estate investor, a stronger source, because of the hundreds and thousands of connections from the club.

I said yes to partnering with Brad and learned more in one year than the 19 years combined. Partnering with a billionaire on a deal, being a co-general partner on 174 units, Limited Partner on 348 units, building relationships. And it's only the beginning.

I said yes, to partnering with a Global Branding and Communications company. One more way to connect internationally and bring value to anyone I encounter.

I said yes to the opportunity to speak on a live stage in Miami and cannot wait for many more global stages. That little girl is jumping from joy.

I have said yes to all these opportunities, and you all may think I have brought value, even if a little to all my relationships, and that it is true, but the winner here, is Me. No matter how much I give, I continue to receive so much more. They are the reason I show up, they are the reason I thrive. They honor me with a privilege to continue to do better in the world. I want to thank every single person who has contributed to my success so far and I am looking forward to reaching as many lives as possible to continue to inspire and I cannot wait to get to know myself better daily. What about you? What do you do?

With gratitude Migena

And remember, always express to influence. We touch lives not only through our actions, smiles, and how we show for ourselves.

Get up, dress up, show up!

Migena Agaraj

Global Focused Connector, Business matchmaker, Founder & CEO,10X Business Advisor Trainer & Mentor, TV Host, Public Speaker and Author.

I was born and raised in Fire, Albania. Moved to New York City in 2003. I live with my parents and my brother in the Bronx.

Graduated from Hunter college with an economics degree, double minored in Italian and history.

Fluent in five languages. Twenty + years of experience in customer service. I started my career in real estate over a decade ago as a human resources recruiter. On the same year I was promoted as a supervisor. A year later promoted as project manager for the headquarters of Goldman Sachs. I was an Area Director for a Global Billion-dollar company for over 20 million square feet of space in the Tri-State area. Also, Director of business development for a billion-dollar company. Today, I am the founder and CEO of Eagles MA LLC, a consulting company providing real estate solutions. I am a conduit and business matchmaker. A best-selling author, public speaker, 10X, business advisor, mentor, and trainer. TV host and associate Director for the investment TV show, America's Real Deal. Capital raiser through syndication. Passive and active investor, committee member at Kids for Kids, an NYC organization raising for Saint Jude's Children's Hospital, Director for Global Partnerships for a Branding and Commutations company.

I love to connect, collaborate and create friendships, partnerships & opportunities on a global scale. I love to travel, play golf, cook and enjoy being a guest on Podcasts.

Migena can be reach at:
> *askmigena.com* and *PowerfulFemaleImmigrants.com*